Life's
Fingerprint

Life's Fingerprint

Your Birth Order

How Birth Order Affects Your Path Throughout Life

■ ■ ■

Dr. Robert V. V. Hurst

PBO Press
Permissions Department
P.O. Box 1790
Mandeville, LA 70470-1790

ISBN: 978-0-97913-610-8
LCCN: 2007942878
                    10 9 8 7 6 5 4 3 2 1

Printed in the United States of America by PBO Press.

www.lifesfingerprint.com

■ ■ ■

This book is dedicated to Catherine Breslin Carlson, my mentor of many years. She taught me to look at life and people from a completely different perspective, understanding that many parts of a person's life and character are not of their making.

CONTENTS

PREFACE

My life as an orthodontist is regulated by school holidays. That's when everyone thinks they want to see me—until something better comes along. (It doesn't take much to top a dental appointment.) I've grown accustomed to being in the office during the school holidays of Christmas, New Year's, Easter, and spring break, but the week of the Fourth of July is different. This is when I hear from many of the patients I treated long ago. Being alone in the office during this week is always an enlightening experience for me.

On one of these days the front page of our local newspaper featured an article titled, "Head Custodian Taking Break after 37 Years." It seems that James Spencer, the oldest of nine children, began work at the school at age sixteen after his father died and he had to help his mother with the bills. He continued to work while he got his high school diploma and then became head custodian, overseeing a staff of ten people. His job started at seven in the morning, but he was always early, and always in control of his duties and staff. He was absent only once during the thirty-seven years— the day his mother died. This was his first and only job.

This story illustrates some characteristics of the first-born child better than any example I can think of, and there it was on the front page of the paper. This man was the head of his team, dependable and responsible. Only a first-born would keep the same job for thirty-seven years and be there for his mother in life and in death.

Later that day, I attended to all the calls that came in while I was out. My secretary, Anne, neatly arranged all the messages by the name of the caller, nature of the problem, phone number, and what was said to them. She then color-coded them for my action. Anne worked with me for over thirty years and was the super-organized and reliable only child. She liked to be home during the week of the Fourth of July. Her family was central to her life, which is a characteristic of only children. This Fourth of July was especially important because her daughter, son-in-law, and three grandchildren were arriving from Africa for a long-overdue visit. The fact that her daughter and son-in-law are third-born and fourth-born children is not surprising.

Third children, as adults, see life very differently than do the other birth orders. Their view of life is more altruistic, and giving themselves to the service of God makes Anne's daughter's missionary work in Africa a natural calling. The fourth-born, her son-in-law, loves the adventure of Africa. Having fun while someone else carries the heavy load is a fourth-born trait. In this case it's left to his wife.

I walked back into the lab area and found a do not touch note on some unfinished lab work that my lab tech, Ellen, had left. It shouldn't surprise me that as a second-born, Ellen did not want anyone messing up "her" space, or for that matter, telling her what to do. I knew better and left everything alone.

I began to tackle the twenty-one messages that needed my attention. First there was Scott, whom I had treated eight years ago, and who had a broken retainer. Scott is a first-born. He works in investment banking, following in his father's footsteps. It is not unusual for the first-born son to follow in his dad's path.

When I told Scott I could fix his retainer, I could hear his sigh of relief. One message returned, twenty to go. Next was Rebecca's mom, who saw a dark spot on the inside of Rebecca's back molar and was sure it was causing her pain. (Rebecca is an only child. Mom is a single parent.) Returning the call, I got Rebecca on the phone. She told me she wasn't having any pain; she was just bored at home. "Why me?" I asked myself. And just how did Mom see way back to the inside of the molar anyway? Never underestimate the power of observation by an only child's mother.

I was dreading the next call, not because of the problem, but because of the parents. Little Sara was manipulating her divorced parents. Sara had a brother five years older and she was daddy's little princess. She has the charm and engaging personality of a second-born, but because of the wide gap in age between her and her brother, she has less fear of adults—like an only child. Dad says she's tough enough to compete with any boy, but to Mom, she's a dainty little girl who can do no wrong. Returning the call, I found she was with Mom this week, and the "glue" had come off a brace in the front of her mouth. "Why didn't you glue it on right?" demanded Mom. Talking with Sara, I found she was playing baseball with the boys, missed a foul ball, and it hit her in the mouth. She wasn't wearing her mouthguard....oops!

My next call was to the father of a patient I hadn't seen in five years. Seems his daughter, Courtney, is now in Alaska doing environmental research and had lost her retainer. (Retainers are a great way for me to keep in touch!) I told him it would be best for her to see an orthodontist in Alaska, since the molds of her mouth are five years old and couldn't be used. Courtney is a third-born, so does it surprise me that she has decided to do environmental research? Not one bit.

One of my last messages was from Dave, my auto mechanic, who really thinks of himself as an artist. One day he said, "See the grease on my hands? I'm the Picasso of grease and this is my paint." I must mention that his garage floor is cleaner than mine, and I don't repair cars. Dave and his wife, who also works at the garage, are people who love what they do, have fun together, and are both third-borns. The last time I visited his garage, he was playing a computer game and was going for a high score. Everyone just waited until he was done before work began again. Dave loves to say, "Do you want it done right or done right now?" I'll let him do it right.

Just then the front door buzzer rang and there stood Ashley. It's been nine years since she graduated from high school and I have only seen her once since, about six years ago. She was one of several students who worked in the office after school. Ashley has an older brother she lived with until she was nine years old. At that time, her parents divorced and she lived with her mom and stepdad. Her brother stayed with her dad. This change made Ashley more of an only child from the age of nine. Having started life as a second child, she now carried the outgoing characteristics and the need to control her own space of the second child, and the strength and no fear of authority of the only child. In the office, she never wanted to be back in the clinic with the patients, but at the front desk meeting and greeting everyone.

Ashley said she had brought her boyfriend home with her. At twenty-nine years old, living a thousand miles away from home, she has carved out her own life. She has had many boyfriends, but in her words, "No one will treat me the way I need to be treated."

"Like a princess?" I asked.

"Right," she said. "They just don't seem to get it. The guy I brought home is thirty-four years old and has been married before. We dated for awhile and then broke up. He then comes crawling back to me, saying he just can't live without me. Now I just have to figure out how to get him to do everything my way and think it's his idea." (Is this a universal concept?)

I'm always interested in what line of work my former patients get comfortable with after college. I asked Ashley what she was doing now. "Selling diamonds," she said. "I can sell to anyone, it's really unbelievable! My boss says he has never promoted anyone as fast as me, nor has he seen anyone sell like me." Little does he know that Ashley is a princess, and what better place for her than at a diamond retailer? Her boyfriend better get ready....I think she's got him now.

As you can see, birth order, life's fingerprint, is all around us. If we understand the characteristics of these birth order positions, then we can more easily understand ourselves, our life's path, and the people in our lives.

INTRODUCTION

Why Study Birth Order?

If you have just picked up this book, I'm sure the title got your attention. Some of you will say, "No way does my order of birth determine who I am." Others will agree with me that their order of birth and interaction with their siblings really does determine who they are. As you read on, you'll find out more about the different birth orders. You'll notice that it's not just a coincidence that similar birth orders have similar personality traits. You'll see that each successive child in a family tries to be different, and that difference is seen in all families and crosses all cultural, racial, and ethnic lines.

This book is written for everyone to use without having a background in psychology—just a background in life. I must tell you that I am not a psychiatrist, nor do I have any formal training in the area of child psychology.

If I'm not a psychologist or psychiatrist, what gives me the credentials to write a book on birth order?

Let me explain. I have been an orthodontist for over thirty-five years. I work with children daily and have to rely on the cooperation of teenagers for my success! Communication and observation are very important in what I do. Often this is the first exposure a preteen or teenager has had to a long term personal commitment to their health. I have found each child to be "birth order" unique in their approach to the care and cooperation with wearing orthodontic appliances. In order to encourage each child with this commitment, I study and then engage their specific personality to get them to take the proper actions.

As an orthodontist, I try to go beyond my patients' teeth and talk to them about their lives. I see my patients at monthly intervals, usually over a two-year period. After that I continue to follow them for life. (Remember, they all have retainers.) In addition, I often get to treat more than one child from each family. That's what started my interest in birth order. I found that although children may come from the same household, there was often *nothing* similar about their personalities or their approach to their orthodontic treatment, often to their parents' dismay.

Why am I writing this book? I hope that parents or future parents who read this book will look at each of their children differently. I can't count the number of times I've seen parents try to make all their children alike. They compare them to each other, wanting them to achieve goals that for some children are unattainable or just not important. Each child is different. They all want to be unique in the eyes of their parents, and as such, each sibling has wonderful special talents that should be celebrated for their differences.

The behavior of the child at school, at doctors' appointments, at gymnastics and soccer; what they will do as adults; whom they will marry—all are related to their birth order. With an understanding of birth order, many decisions and interactions in life will be easier and less stressful for both parents and children and anyone who interacts with them.

While working with my patients, I became very interested in the different behaviors that each birth order demonstrated. This led me to begin research on the subject. I have read hundreds of biographies and I always have an eye for birth order information in newspaper and magazine articles. I found the first mention of birth order in the Bible. This was the sibling conflict between Cain and his younger brother, Abel. Cain, the first child of Adam and Eve, was in conflict with Abel. It all came to a head after God accepted Abel's offering above Cain's. The jealous older brother then slew Abel, because, he said, "God loved him best." This became the first recorded case of *siblicide*.

I also found the term *primogeniture*, the practice of giving the castle (if you had one) and the entirety of your wealth, estate, and office or business to the eldest son. Younger sons had to make it on their own.

I couldn't delve into psychology without seeing the name Dr. Sigmund Freud, and, sure enough, he enters the birth order picture. We remember

Cain and Abel

some of his ideas about the child's relationship with his parents. He felt the parental relationship molded children's lives. While he was formulating his ideas, Freud surrounded himself with others working in his field. Among them was a young man named Alfred Adler, who had some very different ideas. In 1902 Freud invited Adler to join his Wednesday Psychological Society, later renamed the Vienna Psychoanalytic Society. Adler was assured by Freud that all ideas would be welcomed. Adler was developing a theory that the child's interaction with his/her siblings was more important than the parents' influence on their personality development.

Freud and Adler parted ways in 1911, each failing to convince the other to accept his point of view, and they never spoke to each other again. Adler left with eight other members of the Psychoanalytic Society and formed his own school. Today he is known as the father of birth order theory. Knowing what we do today about birth order, we realize that the relationship between Freud and Adler was doomed from the start. For you see, while Freud was the first child in his father's second family, Adler was a second child. Adler would not give in to Freud, who was acting the role of a number-one child and thus treated like a "king" by his family.

Alfred Adler

Freud was used to giving orders and having them followed. Adler, as a second-born, would not have liked to be told what to do.

WHY IS THIS BOOK ON BIRTH ORDER DIFFERENT THAN THE OTHERS?

A One, a Two, and a Three

If only birth order identification were as easy as 1-2-3. Unfortunately, it isn't. Just because you were the first-born or second-born doesn't automatically give you a set of predetermined personality characteristics. There are many other factors that must be considered. This book addresses the factors that others have not.

We will deal with some of these in the section on finding your *true* birth order. The critics of birth order theory (and there are many) rightly contend that the ordinal number of your birth does not always relate to that number's birth order characteristics. The critics say that birth order is an overly simplistic method to predict such a complicated subject as personality development. They argue that birth order theory doesn't take into consideration, for example, what happens when many years separate children in their own families. That's the reason for this book: to show you how birth order really works when you factor in the many variables.

Although there have been other books written on birth order, to my knowledge, most have been written by therapists. They counsel families and children who come to them with problems and are unable to function for one reason or another. I have had the opportunity to see functioning children in the real world on a day-to-day basis, adjusting to life and its challenges. I have seen the expression of their birth orders throughout this thirty-five-year period. What I have learned is that you can't treat all children the same. This should be the advice given to all doctors, teachers, parents, coaches, and all others who work with children.

I am now seeing the children of my first patients who came to me when I started practicing. Although there are similar family characteristics, these children's birth order characteristics far outweigh the family influence. Because I have been able to see so many families, I will also discuss the effect of gender and its position in the sibling birth order of families with multiple children.

Unique to this book is the discussion of double birth orders and families within families. Double birth order occurs when four or more years separate siblings, especially when there is a four-year grade difference at school. This concept is the Rosetta stone of understanding birth order theory, and it is why just your ordinal birth order, or number order of birth, is sometimes not your *real* birth order. Without an understanding of double birth orders, birth order theory has a very poor reliability.

Throughout this book I will use examples of famous actors, politicians, characters in movies and television sitcoms, cartoon characters, and criminals. I will also use stories about my own friends, family, and patients to show you the characteristics of the different birth orders. I use these examples because these are people we all know. For instance, did you know that Bill Clinton and Monica Lewinsky have similar birth orders?

BIRTH ORDER IS NOT THE COMPLETE EXPLANATION OF HUMAN BEHAVIOR

Human behavior is a very complex subject. Experts have been debating the effects of nurture (the environment) versus nature (genes or genetic potential) for years, without resolution. Birth order encompasses components of both. Nurture represents the home environment: mom, dad, siblings, and their interactions. Nature, the gene pool, is the mix of genetic factors affecting overall development.

This book is not meant to debate this issue or have *all* the answers. The goal is to give the reader information to better evaluate his own behavior and the behavior of others by understanding the various birth orders.

HOW BIRTH ORDER INFORMATION
IS ORGANIZED IN EACH CHAPTER

An explanation of each birth order is based on the characteristics seen in each order during childhood. Next, examples will be given or stories told that emphasize these characteristics. It's important to note that all birth orders manifest themselves in two seemingly dissimilar ways. I'm sure you know someone who can be shy in some situations, yet outgoing in others. All birth orders have two sides to them.

In order to illustrate the birth order characteristics, I will use people we all know who demonstrate these birth order behaviors. For some, I will first give you their names, for others I will tell you a little bit about them and their lives before revealing who they are. This little exercise will help you get a better understanding of the specific birth orders.

You will see that people do not change from childhood to adulthood, and each has a special path in life. Birth order is truly *life's fingerprint*.

1

THE TRADITIONAL BIRTH ORDERS AND THEIR VARIATIONS

TRADITIONAL BIRTH ORDERS

There are five traditional birth orders. Each one gives the owner a different view of life and the people around them. If you are a playful person, you will be the granny on rollerblades when you're eighty. There are many examples in our aging society of the "elderly" not acting their age: we hear of bungee-jumping seventy-year-olds, even parachuting presidents. Our former president George H. W. Bush, an athlete and a second-born, celebrated his eightieth birthday with a parachute jump! People act in sync with their birth orders.

The traditional orders of birth are:

- the only child, who has no other siblings
- the first-born, who starts life as an only child, only to have another child added to the family within three years
- the second-born, who is no more than three years younger than the older sibling

- the third-born, who is no more than three years younger than the next older sibling
- the fourth-born, who is no more than three years younger than the next older sibling

For the traditional birth orders to fit there must be fewer than four school years between each child. With the addition of the fifth child, the birth orders start all over again, but these children show the birth order characteristics with less intensity. (More on this later.)

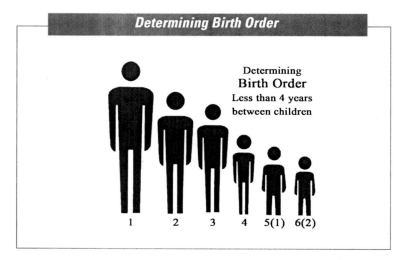

Some of you will want to flip through the book and locate your birth order for a quick read on who you are….Don't do it! There is a lot more involved in locating your real birth order than meets the eye. We will start now with a little questionnaire to find your real birth order.

Your true birth order is determined by the interaction among the brothers and sisters you lived with during your first sixteen years. Because of the high number of divorced and separated parents, family living arrangements can be quite complex. The data from the Annual Social and Economic Supplement to the 2003 Current Population Survey reported that there were 111 million families in the United States. This represented a decrease in the growth rate of new families from 1.7 million per year during the 1970s to only 1.1 million per year in the 1990s. From 1970 to 2003 the proportion of single-mother families grew to 26 percent from only 12 percent. The survey also showed that the proportion of all unmarried partner households has increased from 2.9 percent in 1996 to 4.2 percent in 2003.

When reviewing children's living arrangements, we find that in 2002, 69 percent of all children lived with two parents, 23 percent lived with only their mother, 5 percent lived with only their father, and 3 percent lived in a household with neither parent. This would mean that 31 percent of all children did not live in a home with both parents.

The following questionnaire will help you find your true birth order, which may not be your ordinal number at birth.

FIND YOUR TRUE BIRTH ORDER

1. List in order from oldest to youngest the names and ages of all your natural brothers and sisters. Include yourself and circle your name.

    _____

    _____

    _____

    This will give you your ordinal birth number. If there are four or more years between you and your nearest older and younger sibling (if present), you can add the only birth order to your ordinal one. (1/0, 2/0, 3/0, 4/0, etc.)

    If there is a space of four years between your nearest older sibling and you and all other siblings are less than four years apart, then you are a family within a family (addressed in Chapter Eleven). If you are a child in a family within a family then you can add another ordinal number to your birth order. The first sibling after the four-year gap would add a one. For example, if you were the third-born, have younger siblings, and there were four years between you and your older sibling, then you are a 3/1. Your next sibling would be a 4/2.

2. List in order from oldest to youngest the names and ages of all your stepbrothers and stepsisters. If any stepsiblings lived with you, list them in order by age and then refigure your ordinal birth order.

    _____

_____

_____

3. Which of your natural siblings and which of your stepsiblings did you live with from birth to age sixteen?

_____

_____

_____

4. Did you ever live with adults other than your parents from birth to age sixteen? How many years did you live with these people?

      a) grandparents_____
      b) aunts or uncles_____
      c) close family friends_____
      d) other_____

This information will let you know if you get a new birth order due to separation from your other siblings. It must be a period longer than a year or two to make any difference.

5. If you answered yes to question #4, at what age did you live with these people? Were there other children in the house? If yes, list their ages and yours at the time you lived with them.

_____

_____

_____

6. Were any of your brothers or sisters (including stepbrothers and stepsisters) with whom you lived handicapped either mentally or physically? If so, which ones?

_____

7. Did any of your brothers or sisters die either before you were born or after? If so, which ones and how old were you at their time of death? If they were older than you, move up one number in birth order.

_____

_____

8. Were you adopted or did you have any adopted siblings in the family? Put everyone in order by their age and consider your age or theirs at the time of adoption.

_____

_____

9. Are you a twin or triplet? If so, are you the first-, second-, or third-born? Were there any siblings born before or after you and your twin or triplet? If so, how many years apart?

_____

_____

Perhaps now you can see why skipping to later chapters might not give you the correct answer on your real birth order. Look at the questionnaire you just filled out to determine who you really lived with for the first sixteen years and which birth order you represent. You may have been thrown into a "blended family" with children from two marriages. Your birth order could go up, down, or stay the same. There is no blending of your old and new birth order, as the new family structure is much too powerful. Everyone is expected to assume their special position in this new family. This will be addressed in more depth in the chapter on combined families.

Your birth order can also move up if there is a handicapped child older than you in the family. Another scenario involves children who are pulled out of the family to live with grandparents, which can make this child an only and change the birth order of the other siblings.

OTHER FACTORS

Here are some examples to help with your birth order determination:

Becky was the first-born and was followed by four boys at two-year intervals: Brian, James, Ronald, and Jeff. At the age of three, after her second-born brother, Brian, came into the family, Becky went to live with her grandparents for the rest of her childhood. This changed everyone's

Birth Order Change List		
	Before	After
Becky	1	0
Brian	2	1
James	3	2
Ronald	4	3
Jeff	5	4

birth order. In living with her grandparents, Becky became an only child. Brian moved into the number-one position, James the number-two, Ronald the number-three, and Jeff the number-four.

Combined families offer a more complicated pattern. Jodie, age nine, was an only child when her mother married a widower with three children: Molly, age fourteen; Christie, age twelve; and Robbie, age eight. What happened to their birth orders? Molly stayed a one; Christie stayed a two; Jodie lost her only status and as a nine-year-old got demoted to the three position; and Robbie moved down to a four. If Jodie is very resistant to her change in status, there will be a lot of friction in this new blended family. This is how it might sound: "Jodie isn't adjusting well. But Molly and Christie are doing just fine." Well, Molly and Christie didn't have to change birth orders in this new family, but Jodie had an enormous demotion. The little guy Robbie, although also demoted, only moved down one spot. But because he is still the only boy in the family, he holds on to his special status.

Birth Order Change List			
		Before	After
Jodie	9yr	0	3
Molly	14yr	1	1
Christie	12yr	2	2
Robbie	8yr	3	4

When a handicap occurs, changes also occur in the birth order. In another example, Bradley is age eleven. Alan is age nine, and was born with a severe learning disability. Aaron is age eight and is moved up to the number-two position, moving Alan down to the number-three position, because of his learning disability. Aaron's dad described Aaron as the "animal" because of his aggressiveness and his move up to the number-two position.

Birth Order Change List			
		Before	After
Bradley	11yr	1	1
Alan	9yr	2	3
(Disability)			
Aaron	8yr	3	2

What happens when a sibling dies? (Question #7 on our survey.) We are all familiar with the Kennedy family. We know that John's older brother was killed in World War II. This moved John, a number two, into the number one position. Later he became president of the United States, fulfilling the dream that his father had for his older brother. Although he moved up to the first-born position, he still retained the engaging personality traits of the second-born. That may be why he was the favorite of the press corps.

THE PHANTOM CHILD

We can't leave the subject of the death of a sibling without mentioning the phenomenon of the phantom child. This is a child whose premature death is never really accepted by the family. There are two types of phantom children: those who die shortly after birth and those who die later in childhood. This child remains in the family, so to speak, and presents an insurmountable problem to the other siblings. This phantom child may be portrayed as perfect in every way and is an example of perfection that the other siblings can never achieve. This effect of an older child dying later in adolescence may have had an effect on Richard Milhous Nixon—a person with a complex life whom you will see again in a later chapter.

Richard Nixon

Nixon had an older brother who died of tuberculosis as a young adult. Nixon moved up in birth order to the number-one position, but had to work very hard to measure up. What a powerful event for Richard Nixon, and a possible reason for his over-achievement.

Vincent Willem Van Gogh was born March 30, 1853, one year almost to the day from the death of his brother, who lived only one week. Vincent was given the name of his deceased brother. It was said that his mother never got over the death of her first-born child. Vincent led a troubled life, afflicted with recurring bouts of mental illness that culminated in his suicide. Could this phantom brother have been a contributing factor?

You, of course, will have to evaluate the effect of any sibling who died in your family and decide if it had the phantom child effect.

TWINS AND TRIPLETS AND OTHER MULTIPLE BIRTHS

The question concerning twins or triplets or any multiple births is a tricky one. These children take on their birth order characteristics just as soon as they know their order, but may "sense" their order very soon after birth. I treated twin boys of a family who lived down the street from me. I would regularly drive the boys to the office for the first appointment of the day. These boys were identical and they could never understand how I knew Jimmy from Joey. Well, it was easy! Jimmy, the first-born twin, always took the front passenger seat, making Joey sit in the back.

The additional problem with multiple births in any family is that they take so much time, energy, and family resources that they may completely throw off the normal sequence of the family birth orders. For example, if the birth of twins comes several years after the birth of the first child, the older child may not get the attention that he normally would from his parents because of the extra time necessary for the twins. The first-born would definitely feel shortchanged and this would affect his behavior.

SPACING BETWEEN SIBLINGS

One final and very important consideration in finding your true birth order in our questionnaire is the spacing between siblings. When four years or more (or at least four school years) come between individual siblings, the older sibling carries a double birth order—that of an only and their ordinal, or order number of birth.

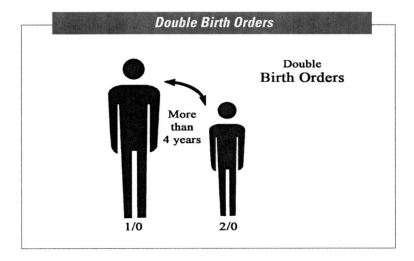

If the second sibling is at least four years younger than his older sibling and has no younger siblings within four years, then this second child also has a double birth order, that of an only, and his ordinal number of birth, two. We will get into this area in greater detail later in the book in the chapters on double birth orders.

THE STRENGTH OF THE BIRTH ORDERS

There are no "bad" birth orders. Each has its strengths and weaknesses—but there is a definite power hierarchy. Do you remember the game Rock, Paper, Scissors? The two players start with clenched fists and on the count of three either open their hands (paper), keep their hands closed (rock), or spread two fingers (scissors). The paper covers the rock, the scissors cuts the paper, the rock breaks the scissors: each has its strength. The same is true of birth orders—they each have their strengths and weaknesses.

As a general rule, the higher the birth order, the more power there is over a lower birth order. A first-born has greater power than a second-born and the second-born has more power than a third-born. Power is a relative thing, because each child uses his unique birth order characteristics to get noticed, or claim victory over an older brother or sister. The older sibling will cry "foul," because the younger sibling will be using a technique that the older would never dream of using.

2

SUPERMAN WAS
AN ONLY CHILD

THE ONLY CHILD

THE ONLY #0

It's been nine long months, and the expectant parents have been planning for the arrival of their first-born almost from the moment of conception. Their bonding with this child and his bonding with his parents will be unique. As an only child he represents the ego of his parents, their representative to the world. They have already put him on the waiting list for the very best school in town, baby gymnastics, and baby story time. The photo album already has pictures of his pregnant mother and his first ultrasound. The grandparents are more excited than mom and dad at the arrival of their first grandchild. Does any of this sound familiar?

I know one only child whose parents moved to the same town she moved to after her marriage. They then moved again when she and her

Characteristics of an Only Child
▪ Wants to please parents
▪ Self-confident
▪ Not afraid of adults
▪ Can be a miniature adult
▪ May be spoiled
▪ Says, "I can do it myself"

husband transferred to another location. The only child is destined to take care of both parents later in life, which can be a real burden on his own family. This child has been well prepared for the task, however, and he feels it's payback time for all the care his parents gave him.

I can always tell when an only child comes to the office—both parents will accompany the child and will not stay in the waiting area, needing to be with their child at all times. The parents confer with the child concerning his treatment, and need permission from him to proceed, just like an adult. Sometimes these children seem to have control over their parents.

You can already sense the positive characteristics of the only child. They are very "adult-like"—after all, adults are their peer group. The parents can spend a lot of time nurturing these children because they outnumber him, two parents to one child. This child does not have to compete for attention in the family: he is the main event! The flipside of this is that, being the center of attention, he has to perform to please his parents; it's not easy to escape two concerned adults.

As children, onlies appear to develop a conservative nature. This is relative, because they are really representing their parents' generation. This reflection of the "older" generation endears them to their teachers, and their classmates look to them for guidance. They usually are elected class president and are always the one selected to "go ask the teacher." These are very serious children; you won't find them playing like other children. As they've never had to share their toys, this can be a problem. Their parents have the biggest impact on their lives, and the only child absorbs and combines the birth order characteristics of both his parents. This gives each only child his own "only" flavor.

What's His Name?

His father was a dentist, but he never really connected with him. His father's drinking problem complicated matters. His mother was very possessive of her only son and relied on him for everything—especially after his parents divorced in 1935. He went to college on his dime but had to drop out for financial reasons. He was a serious student and a gentleman of the press, always appearing very adult-like. We can't forget "the most trusted man in America." I'm sure you got this one as Walter Leland Cronkite Jr., the dean of all news broadcasters.

Movies are a good way to see birth order in action. In the movie *Willy Wonka & the Chocolate Factory*, we see the two types of only children. In the movie, five children won the "golden ticket" to take a special tour of Wonka's chocolate factory.

Charlie was the adult-like only child, very supportive to his extended family. Augustus, Mike, Veronica, and Violet were the "spoiled" only children. The theme throughout the movie was that the children were a product of the mother and father's upbringing, which in the case of onlies is true.

The absence of other siblings often remains a mystery for the only child. All the explanations by his parents, such as, "We only have enough love for one child," or "The pregnancy was so difficult we couldn't have any more children," are rarely any comfort to the only child. He still wonders why he doesn't have any brothers or sisters. Sometimes onlies feel responsible and try to "make it up" to their parents by giving them lots of grandchildren. As adults, only children seem to have a love of family and family life. This could be because as children they always felt something was missing in their own lives when they saw their friends with brothers and sisters.

If they can't have a family of children, they often opt for pets. It's not uncommon for them to have multiple dogs and cats. They can't seem to deny their pets a sibling. We find this true with our only children patients when we ask them about their pets; they all seem to come in twos.

In the adult world, the well-adjusted only child has no fear. He can blaze new trails in starting a business, leading a company, or facing the public. He is not afraid to make the "big" decisions, as most onlies have been instilled with lots of self-confidence.

As with all birth orders, there is a flip side. Some over-protected onlies become timid, shy, and very introverted. Having been protected by their parents, "onlies" can lack well-developed social skills. Their best friend can be a book, which keeps them alone and even more isolated from other children. They have great difficulty "reading" other children, as they see them from the viewpoint of an adult in their parents' generation. They want to control their friends and be their center of attention. The protection the parents have for this only child will last a lifetime.

Life Stories

Clark Kent/Superman was an adopted only child, who was really a super kid and wanted to make things right in the world. I'm sure he made Mr.

What's His Name?

This comedian and only child has a love of horses, which he learned from his father, who came from Ireland. He even has a comedy routine based on a jockey character. His mother taught him to sew and he still makes some of his clothes. Known for his deadpan humor, he has a hard time showing emotion in public. While in charge of troop placements in the Army, he "misplaced" a battalion of seventy-five soldiers, not typical for an organized only child. His family is so important to him that after his divorce, he moved only one block away from the family so he could be with his six children. Who is he? None other than Tim Conway.

and Mrs. Kent very proud. He is portrayed as very serious and never displays much of a sense of humor. (You would have to have a lot of self-confidence to wear red and blue tights and a cape, even if they were made by your mother.)

Christopher Reeves, who played the hero in the original *Superman* series, was an only child. How is that for perfect typecasting?

Comedians as Only Children

Jack Benny, the violin-playing comedian, was an only child who had a kind of dry, deadpan, adult humor. His ability to play the violin speaks volumes for the influence of his mother on his after-school activities.

Tony Randall, from the long-running comedy *The Odd Couple*, certainly had a very dry sense of humor. His lifelong interest in opera, antiques, paintings, and classical music are what parents would be proud of in their only child.

Betty White, one of the Golden Girls, is another only child comedian. She is known for her "cutting" remarks that seem to come from nowhere. She loves game shows, something she practiced with her parents while growing up. As with most only children, her parents were her friends. When she married Allen Ludden in 1963 she became the stepmother to four children. She was perhaps seeking the large family she may have felt she missed. Then there is the other type of only who either only wants one child or who doesn't want any children at all, as the idea of family seems foreign to them. Birth orders always have two points of view that on the surface seem opposite. Looking deeper, much of the onlies behavior will be a reflection of the birth orders of their parents. This is the *only* birth order that is not influenced by sibling interaction, as the dominant force in the only child's life is the parents. I know several onlies where both parents were second-borns and these onlies have many traits in common with number two children. It is not the scope of this book to get into the nuances or fine tuning of birth order interpretation. However, this parental influence factor must be noted in relation to only children. This is why onlies come in a variety of flavors.

Charles Shultz, an only child and the author of the *Peanuts* comic strip, had a fascination with family and children all his life, having five children of his own. His characterizations of his comic strip children were right on for their birth orders.

Only children who became entertainers or actors

John Uhler Lemmon, III, changed his name to Jack Lemmon and had the distinction of being born in an elevator. He said he knew at age eight or nine that he wanted to be an actor. Nothing stood in his way. His fellow actors said he was fearless and not easily intimidated.

Laura Bush

Frank Sinatra, an only child, was known as the Chairman of the Board. He was almost always in control and showed little fear of the establishment.

Brooke Shields started acting at a very early age, showing the adult-like qualities it takes to be a successful child actress. Her protective mother was always waiting in the wings.

First Lady Laura Bush is an only child. Her husband is always saying what a great support she is to him. It is interesting to note that her first job was that of a teacher and school librarian—books are many times an only child's best friend. As First Lady she has been instrumental in restoring the school libraries in the aftermath of Hurricane Katrina in New Orleans and the Gulf Coast of Mississippi.

Drew Barrymore, child actress and part of the legendary Barrymore family, can fit the role of a spoiled only child at times. We have followed her through her role in *E.T.*, her two marriages, and her outrageous behavior on the *Late Show with David Letterman*, when she lifted up her shirt as a birthday present to Dave. Even as a child actress she would talk like an adult, which endeared her to the audience.

Sometimes the overprotective parents of an only child can go too far in their indulgence. The story is told of the only child who was very slow to speak. His parents took him to all the specialists and none could find anything wrong with him. Then one day he said, "The dam oatmeal is cold." His parents were ecstatic. "He's speaking!" they said in unison. "Why haven't you spoken up until now?" they asked. Their son replied, "Up until now, everything was okay." This might be pushing the idea of the parents' indulgence of an only child a little far, but it makes the point.

As adults, only children have a hard time denying themselves anything. This can affect shopping trips, personal relationships, and their business sense. Where did this all begin? During their childhood, mom and dad could and would give them anything they wanted, and for some this carried over into their adult life.

William Randolph Hearst was an example of this attitude. As a child, he was given anything he wanted. His father, George Hearst, was a miner who made his fortune from the Ontario silver mine, the Anaconda silver and copper mine, and the Homestake gold mine. His father said, "What Willie wants, Willie gets." All his life William Randolph Hearst went on buying trips throughout Europe, bringing back and storing everything imaginable. Tapestries, paintings, sculpture, even whole buildings with each stone numbered so he could put them back together at home! The Hearst Castle in California is a testament to his buying trips. Many of the items he acquired abroad were used in its construction, and many more ended up in storage. His publishing empire is still going strong with the many newspapers and magazines he bought during his lifetime.

What's His Name?

This only child's parents divorced when he was five years old. His mother moved in with her parents, and he got an older extended family. His father was in the financial markets in New York and gave him a book with a very prophetic financial inscription in it. The family was very musical, and he took up the clarinet and saxophone and played professionally in the 1940s. He studied with the same teacher and at the same time as Stan Getz, the famous saxophone player. Precocious, intelligent, well behaved, and polite, this young man was president of his home room in school. (So typical of an only child.) This was the background of the former chairman of the Federal Reserve Board, Alan Greenspan.

The movie *The Aviator* chronicled the life of another only child, Howard Hughes. Hughes used the family fortune to fund his love of flying and movie production. He also used his money to develop and fly some very innovative planes. He built the Spruce Goose, a giant plane made entirely out of wood. It was meant to transport troops in World War II, but the war ended before it could be used. So focused was this only child that when the government ran out of money for this project, he used his own to see it to completion.

We don't see a lot of only children become outstanding team athletes, maybe because of their parents' tendency toward over-protection. Or perhaps because they have no need to compete; they are already the center of attention. The only children who do become athletes usually follow in their parents' footsteps, or pick a non-team sport.

Tiger Woods is an example of an only child following his father's dream. The youngest golfer ever to win the Masters, Tiger was influenced by his father, who started teaching him the moment he was old enough to swing a club. Tiger, of course, would want to please his parents and succeed. Golf is not really a team sport, and is certainly not a contact sport, but it's one that takes a lot of mental discipline—something at which an only child would excel.

Only children are very good at handling criticism and overcoming great odds to do their "own" thing. Charles Lindbergh, nicknamed the "Lone Eagle," showed the confidence of the only child when he made the first nonstop solo flight across the Atlantic Ocean. This only child also liked to make his own rules. In addition to his five children with his wife, he had three more children with a woman in Germany. This information came out only after his and the German woman's deaths, as she wanted to protect the name of her children's famous father.

The next time you want a copy of a document, you have another only child to thank. Chester Floyd Carlson, born February 8, 1906, was the inventor of the xerography process. He did not come from a background of scientists but was the son of a barber and a housekeeper. They instilled in him the confidence that comes from being an only child: to just go ahead with his dreams.

Some only children use their strengths and great organizing ability in nefarious ways. Joe Bonanno, the famous Mafia boss and godfather, was born in Sicily into an old family with great traditions. He was an orphan by the time he was a teenager, but had briefly lived in America as a child. He then returned to America to pursue a life in the world of organized crime. He was one of only a few Mafia leaders to die a natural death.

FINAL THOUGHTS ON ONLIES #0

When assessing an only child's birth order, look at his parents to see which one he mimics. Remember, you are dealing with an adult and not a child, no matter what his age. This person could appear to be in an "older" generation because that is his peer group. The only can be very organized and self-confident. He can come in two flavors: the responsible adult or the spoiled, overindulged, self-centered person. Onlies by definition are the first-born, but have special characteristics all their own. They can only have the qualities of a first-born when another child is added to the family and they lose their only position. For some children this can be a stressful experience.

Onlies

Alan Alda	J. Paul Getty	Gregory Peck
Lance Armstrong	Tipper Gore	Suzanne Pleshette
Dr. Robert Atkins	Alan Greenspan	Lisa Marie Presley
Lauren Bacall	Andy Griffith	Richard Pryor
Drew Barrymore	Fred Gwynne	Tony Randall
James Beard	Anthony Hopkins	Robert Redford
Jack Benny	Lena Horne	Robert Reed
Ingrid Bergman	Howard Hughes	Condoleezza Rice
Claus Von Bülow	Jesse Jackson	Mickey Rooney
Laura Welch Bush	Elton John	Franklin D. Roosevelt
Chester Carlson	Jack Lemmon	Dutch Schultz
Jackie Chan	Jerry Lewis	Brook Shields
Eric Clapton	Charles Lindbergh	Frank Sinatra
Jimmy Connors	Charles Manson	Joseph Stalin
Tim Conway	James Mansfield	Ivana Trump
David Copperfield	Ann-Margret	Queen Victoria
Walter Cronkite	Edward McMahon	Dr. Ruth Westheimer
James Dean	Ethel Merman	Betty White
Sandra Dee	Roger Moore	Henry Winkler
Phyllis Diller	Harriet Nelson	Jonathan Winters
Peter Falk	Sir Issac Newton	Tiger Woods
Sarah Michelle Gellar	Al Pacino	

3

BORN TO RULE

The First-Born

OF COURSE I GET ALL THE ATTENTION, I'M THE OLDEST

Excitement about the first-born crosses all cultural lines—as I found out with a little language research. Most languages have a special word for the first-born. In German it's *Stammhalter*, in French it's *aine*, in English it's *heir*, in Spanish it's *primicio*, in Norwegian it's *foerstefoedte*, and in Icelandic it's *erfingi*. You might say first-borns are special all around the world.

> **Characteristics of a First-Born**
>
> - Wants to please parents
> - Usually does very well in school
> - Likes to be in charge
> - Likes giving orders to others
> - Very responsible
> - Conservative

---

[1]If you are a second-born your name will be Made, Nengah, or Kadek. The third-born only has two choices, Nyoman or Komang. The fourth-born is always called Ketut. The fifth child starts the name cycle all over again with the addition of the name Balik to Wayan, Gede, or Putu. Balik means first again or to the second power. Stillborn children are also named for their sequence in the family's birth order.

Some cultures go so far as to give one of several names to all children with the same birth order. In Bali, Indonesia, if you are a first-born you will be named Wayan, Gede, or Putu depending on the region in Bali.[1]

Families put a lot of effort into rearing the first-born, especially if he's a boy. It was not Moses who brought the tenth and final plague to the pharaoh of Egypt, but God Himself. This final plague that "all the first-born in the land of Egypt shall die" was the final blow to the pharaoh, and it allowed the Israelites to leave Egypt. Who better than God to know the importance of the first-born in any family?

THE FIRST-BORN OF SEVERAL CHILDREN #1

A first-born will want to please his parents and do things right. He will usually develop into a very self-confident child. He will have respect for adults and their authority. On the negative side, if overindulged, spoiled, and unrestricted, first-borns may become undisciplined, outspoken, and argumentative.

This child starts life as an only child, so he shares many of the same qualities, but not at the same intensity, nor does he have the same level of self-confidence. First-borns do share a conservative outlook with the only child, and reflect, though not so clearly, the attitudes of their parents. More than half of our U.S. presidents have been first-borns, and twenty-one of our original twenty-three astronauts were first-borns. (They are very good at following rules.) When we look at our leaders we find lots of number ones. As I write this, our current president, George W. Bush, and his vice president, Dick Cheney, are both first-borns.

Let's explore the dynamics of the first-born birth order position. Before the second child is born, the intense focus of both parents is on the first-born. Shortly before the second-born comes into the world, the first-born knows there's a change coming. Everything changes for this child. As the parents prepare for the next child, they can no longer give the first-born their undivided attention. This is where the years of separation between each birth make a critical difference. When the spacing of the first two children is a year or less there is, at first, a less perceived threat to the first-born by the second-born. If the second child is born *within two to three years* of the first-born, the older child immediately feels the loss of parental attention: "How can they possibly ignore ME in favor of that crying, annoying little brother or sister?" When the separation between siblings is *four or more years*, the perceived threat to this child's position is diminished. We will discuss this aspect of child spacing and its effect on each child in greater detail with the next birth order, the one/only. When the spacing of the first two children is a year or less, the perceived threat to the first-born by the second-born grows stronger when they get older, as babies they are much less aware of each other.

In the orthodontic office, the first-born children don't really have a lot to say, for they respect authority and will be quite cooperative, following the wishes of their parents by being a "good" boy or girl. As they are usually the first child to do everything in the family, the pressure is on them to do the right thing so as not to cause trouble or embarrass their parents. Since the parents invest a lot of their ego in the first-born, they view this child's behavior personally.

What does the addition of the second child really do to the self-confidence of the first-born? The first-born feels a little insecurity—the enemy is *within*, so to speak—and he is not equipped to handle this intruder into his world. He has had no experience with competition; up until now he was alone. A degree of resentment and the feeling that something is lost takes place. This gives rise to a lingering doubt and a loss of self-confidence.

J. K. Rowling, the author of the Harry Potter books, has a sister, Dianne, who is two years younger. Rowling has said, "I showed confidence to the world, but inside I was feeling utterly incompetent." This feeling would be normal, but for some, difficult to overcome. For others it gives them the drive to overachieve.

When left alone with their younger siblings, first-borns like to take over their parents' role. More than anything, first-borns want to please their parents and

What's Her Name?

She was the first-born in the family and had two younger brothers. She grew up in a very conservative home. Her brothers said she was very competitive and always wanted to be in control. As a little girl she was very headstrong and many times refused to obey her mother. She won the Miss South Dakota beauty pageant. She is Mary Hart, co-host of *Entertainment Tonight*.

do the right thing. Unlike the situation of the only child, there are others in line who want the attention of mom and dad and are looking for their opening if number one slips up. The first-born has a power struggle on his hands after the birth of the second-born, and has to decide with which parent to identify. He usually will pick the parent that he perceives has the greatest power, usually his father.

In our complex society, with its unclear roles, either parent could be the more powerful in the family. This creates a tremendous amount of tension in the first-born, especially if the threat to his throne is real. He is the "leader of the pack" to his brothers and sisters. To keep his position, he proceeds cautiously but is always mindful of adult authority. This child, if a boy, will really feel the loss of his father in a divorce situation. He now feels called upon to take his father's role in the family and, if very young, will find this new role very difficult.

When interacting with their peer group, first-borns usually want to take the lead. Other children may see them as bossy, always trying to get their way. The oldest child sees himself as the enforcer of mom's, dad's, or the teacher's rules.

In one of the *Peanuts* comic strips, Lucy, the oldest, says to Linus, her younger brother, "You are my younger brother and I'm your older sister, and that's the way it's going to be all the days of your life....and don't tell me you never think about it." Linus's comment about Lucy says it all: "Big sisters are the crab grass in the lawn of life!"

If there is nothing else to remember about one type of first-born, it is that they love to take charge and give orders. After all, they have had a lot of practice with their brothers and sisters. They sometimes don't understand why others don't follow their orders. Who really has the right to disobey the king or queen?

PEANUTS reprinted by permission of United Feature Syndicate, Inc.

There is another type of first-born child that develops when the parental pressure is too great to bear. This child feels he can't do anything right or his work is just not good enough. This first-born becomes very shy and withdrawn, afraid to make decisions for fear of being wrong. This person can develop into the other type of first-born that does not appear to be "bossy." This is the "I can't help you enough" person, who controls those around him by seemingly selfless caring. You might compare this to the stereotype of the Jewish or Italian mother who says to her grown children, "I worked and slaved for you. Why don't you ever call or visit me?" What a guilt trip this can be!

Because the first-born has younger siblings, this is when *gender* makes a difference, or, I should say, has an effect on the personality of the first-born. This is also the position that is affected most by sibling rivalry when the second sibling wants to move up and take the throne. When this happens, sibling rivalry is central to the personality of this first-born. Physical and gender characteristics, or the Ken and Barbie parameters, are now brought into the equation.

The first-born must protect his or her throne at all costs. The rivalry is usually more obvious between boys. When the oldest is a boy and the number two is a girl, she doesn't have much of a chance to take over the throne unless her older brother really messes up. When the oldest is a girl and the second is a boy, look out for fireworks. This number two has the best chance of unseating his older sister and she must be very strong in order to withstand the attack.

To protect this position, the first-born is usually better in school than the second-born. After all, he was the first to go to school, so this makes him special. If first-borns are very strong and overshadow their younger siblings, no rivalry takes place and the second child may drop out. However, a little competition is good—after all, life is tough. But too much competition can break a child's spirit.

Let's now take a look at the various one/two combinations and how they influence the first-born.

TWO BROTHERS

When the first two children are boys, the competition can get fierce. This is especially true if the second child grows bigger than the first. Strangers may be confused as to who is older after looking at the size of the two boys. This is very tough on the first-born boy. Remember Cain and Abel? Cain just couldn't take being demoted to number two by God. This is an example of the highly competitive first-born as a fighter.

Grandparents are, at times, better observers of their grandchildren than they were of their own children. A friend of mine described the behavior of two of his grandsons who are three years apart, now ages six and three. He said the three-year-old passes by his older brother and punches him as hard as he can, and the older brother just stands there in stunned disbelief. This is just a test by number two to check for weakness in the "throne."

I found that names also make a difference in how children see themselves. I remember a family that had two boys and named the first son William and the second son George Jr., after his dad. Talk about confusion of position and parental affection! To this day, William has not held a steady job. Last I heard, he was studying to become a casino card dealer while his younger brother followed his dad into the family business.

Life Stories

Another family I have followed had two boys who seemed to be doing everything right. Then brother number two started getting bigger than number one, and although both were good students, the second brother was excelling in school. When I would see them during visits to check their retainers, I noticed that number one was sporting orange spiked hair and an earring. Number two, on the other hand, was the stereotypical all-American boy.

SWITCHING BIRTH ORDER POSITIONS

When the competition for the number-one position is won by number two, the positions switch. The dynamic of two brothers working together is seen with the Smothers Brothers musical comedy team, who exploited the topic of sibling rivalry. Tommy is the older, born in 1937, but plays the part of the goof-off, while his younger brother, Dick, born in 1939, plays the more serious straight role. After they are well into their routine, and Tommy has been scolded by his younger brother for messing up, he always comes back with the line, "Yeah, but Mom always liked me best." This is something only a first-born would say to remind his younger brother of his position. (Their parents divorced when the boys were young, so Mom may have been a single parent to the boys for some time.)

Life Stories

A friend of mine is the second of two boys and has done the birth order switch with his older brother. Growing up, he described a normal relationship with his older brother. Later, when in high school, he started to outshine his brother academically and then made the football team. He remembers that problems began when he was in tenth grade and

Mom likes me best

his brother was a senior. His brother developed narcolepsy; he would just fall asleep at any time during the day. He then became very dependent on his younger brother, following him across the country when the younger brother entered the military. The older brother lived with him, even after brother number two got married.

The older of two brothers can be the most gentle of men, and a very nice guy. Maybe it's because his mother made him help her raise his younger brother. Being supportive to mom may be another way the first-born tries to hold off the competition of his younger brother.

An example of this mellow older brother can be seen with the boys in the Gumbel family. Greg, the sportscaster, is the older by three years, and is much more mellow than his younger brother, Bryant the newsman.

Harrison Ford

News broadcaster Tom Brokaw is the oldest of three boys and has written several books about World War II veterans. The first-born usually reflects society's more traditional values and likes to speak with authority.

Actor Harrison Ford is the older of two boys. Look at the roles he has played: Hans Solo in the *Star Wars* trilogy and Indiana Jones in a series of movies. Always the guy in charge and in control, no matter how bad it gets. This is how many first-borns see themselves in life.

If you're born of royal blood, as is Charles of England, being king is your birthright. When his children, William and Harry, were born, they were referred to in the British press as "the heir and the spare." In the royal family, the rivalry issue has been settled by law, but we have already seen Harry, the second-born, acting out a bit. They say he is a fierce competitor and a fearless athlete on the soccer and lacrosse fields. His mother, the late Princess Diana, used to say, "Don't worry about Harry. He will adapt to anything and charm anybody." William, his older brother, is described as a "nice young man" who follows the rules.

Birth order and *gender* affect other royal families around the world. There has been a royal dilemma in Japan over the past forty years; there has been no male heir to the Chrysanthemum Throne, the world's oldest continuous monarchy. On September 6, 2006, everything changed when Princess Kiko gave birth to a baby boy. This defused a succession dilemma for the coming generation of the royal family. According to their law, no woman can inherit the throne. Debate had been sparked to change this 1947 law. The eldest son has a daughter, Aiko. Princess Kiko is married to the second son. Now their son is currently in line to ascend to the throne since the eldest brother's only child is a daughter.

TWO SISTERS

When we have the combination of two girls, they don't seem to be as physically competitive as two boys. It might be just a society thing, or their levels of testosterone. Here is a story of one of my patients, the older of two girls.

Gloria was an honor student in high school. At one point during high school, her younger sister by two years made the cheerleading squad and was also inducted into the honor society. To complicate matters, Gloria was a bit of a "plain Jane" and her younger sister had suddenly developed into a Britney Spears look-alike. That's when Gloria lost all interest in school, nearly dropped out, and just went through the motions until graduation.

After graduation Gloria got pregnant. The father was of another race and socioeconomic level, which upset her family. Talk about getting attention! Maybe she was looking for a family where she could be the leader? Was this a defiant act after her dethroning? Things went from bad to worse, as her parents would not accept the grandchild, even though it was their first. Things seemed to get better when the couple married, but

Gloria's in-laws were also slow to accept her, and she found them more prone to physical violence than her own family. Work was a problem for her new husband. They went on welfare, and Gloria got a job to help support the family. It seemed that her dream of a college education was gone. Her sister is now way ahead of her in school and is now firmly in control of her throne within the family.

Susan was another first-born I was treating. Shortly after she began her treatment, her younger, more athletic sister started treatment as well. I thought it would be interesting to see what would happen between these two girls. Dad was a coach and Mom was a nurse; Dad would bring them in for their appointments. One day Susan came in for her appointment with bandages over her eye and her right knee. It seems she was competing with her sister in a foot race and lost. You have to give her credit for trying to look good in Dad's eyes and hold her position in the family.

What happens when two girls grow up, move away, and have families of their own? Does the sibling rivalry and the quest for the top position in the family go away? Not at all. Here is a real-life story to prove it.

Life Stories

A friend of mine has two daughters who were in competition for their parents' attention as children and still are as adults. They just can't seem to do enough for their parents. Both girls are married to successful men, one on the East Coast and the other on the West Coast. When their folks are out of town, you can bet one or the other daughter had sent the tickets. The race was on for the first grandchild.

These two sisters, Jerri and June, grew up in a loving home. Jerri was a super high achiever. June was not a slouch, but was overshadowed by her older sister. However, Jerri, the first-born, had trouble getting pregnant, and June became way ahead for the first time in their rivalry when she produced the first grandchild. Jerri was working hard and investigated in vitro fertilization. The doctor suggested that maybe her younger sister could become the surrogate mother. When Jerri asked June if she would be willing to be her surrogate mom, what do you think she said? "No way!" June quickly got pregnant again and had a second son. I'm sure there were many other reasons for her refusal, but could sibling rivalry have some bearing on the decision? Jerri was finally successful, but she had lost the race for the first grandchild. Jerri now has three children, one more than her younger sister, and the third child is the first and only girl! Sibling rivalry can last a lifetime!

FIRST-BORN BOY/SECOND-BORN GIRL

When the first-born is a boy and he has a younger sister, he can take on a protective role, especially if he feels no threat to his throne. If he feels a threat, he can fight or simply ignore his younger sister.

Life Stories

Johnny L. Cochran Jr. (O.J. Simpson's murder trial attorney) had two younger sisters, Pearl and Martha Jean. He would certainly become the big brother they could count on.

Jimmy (Maitland) Stewart had two younger sisters, Mary and Virginia. Who wouldn't look up to Jimmy Stewart as a leader, when we see all the roles he played as this sort of person? Everybody loved his onstage persona. He was the same off stage, someone you felt you could trust and know who he was. He's the big brother who did not feel threatened.

FIRST-BORN GIRL/SECOND-BORN BOY

When the first-born is a girl and the second-born is a boy, the competition can be intense, especially when the boy (in the South) is named Hunter! Just like the Japanese royals, we still have a preference for the boy to take the leading role. This attitude gives the boy a natural jump in unseating his sister from the throne. This preference is changing as more families undergo a reversal of traditional roles. If the traditional parental roles are reversed, it would give the sister an edge over her brother.

Life Stories

This family demonstrates the natural advantage of the second-born boy over a first-born girl. The father, a dentist, had encouraged his children to become dentists, which they both did. When the boy became a dentist, the father gave the practice to him. The girl went back to school to specialize, but the thought of her brother in her father's office was a bitter pill. She left her hometown, married, had a child, got divorced, and moved from practice to practice. She had abdicated the throne to her brother, unwillingly, and has yet to find herself.

Hillary Clinton, former First Lady, senator from New York, and former presidential candidate, is an example of how the competition can be won by an overachieving first-born female. She has two younger brothers: Hugh, three years younger, and Tony, seven years younger. We have seen that Hillary is a high achiever. She has weathered the storms of controversy throughout her life and won. Her younger brother Hugh has not unseated her.

The combinations of the genders of the first two children can give you a sense of the dynamics and power of each child's birth order and its effect on his siblings. Of course, there are other influences, which will be discussed later, that also have a direct bearing on sibling relationships.

FINAL THOUGHTS ON THE FIRST-BORN #1

When looking at a first-born, determine the gender of the second child and the years of separation between them. Also, identify the dominant parent, because this is the parent the first-born will want to follow and emulate. This child will usually be better in school than his younger sibling, but remember that he could also be a "dethroned" number one. If this happens, the number one can show very self-destructive personality traits.

First-Borns

John Adams	Clint Eastwood	John McEnroe
Abigail Adams	Albert Einstein	Graham Nash
Muhammad Ali	Carrie Fisher	Tatum O'Neal
Loni Anderson	Henry Fonda	Peter O'Toole
Paul Anka	Harrison Ford	George S. Patton Jr.
James Arness	Henry Ford	River Phoenix
Benedict Arnold	Michael J. Fox	Pablo Picasso
Jessica Biel	Barry Goldwater	Queen Noor
David Bloom	Billy Graham	Anthony Quinn
Humphrey Bogart	Ulysses S. Grant	Christopher Reeve
Pat Boone	Mary Hart	J. K. Rowling
Camilla Parker Bowles	Hugh Hefner	Babe Ruth
Tom Brokaw	Conrad Hilton	Jane Russell
Raymond Burr	Paris Hilton	Colonel Harland Sanders
Cain	Herbert Hoover	Ernest Shackleton
Prince Charles	Don Imus	Tom Smothers
Jimmy Carter	Naomi Judd	Jimmy Stewart
Julia Child	Caroline Kennedy	Fred Stolle
Hillary Clinton	Jackie Bouvier Kennedy	Harry S. Truman
Rosemary Clooney	Henry A. Kissinger	John Walsh
Johnnie Cochran	Evel Knievel	Sam Walton
Sean "Puffy" Combs	Ricki Lake	Raquel Welch
Ann Curry	Gypsy Rose Lee	Adam West
General George Custer	Rush Limbaugh	Prince William
Leonardo da Vinci	Sophia Loren	Bruce Willis
Bo Derek	Shirley MacLaine	Steve Wozniak
Michael Douglas	Barbara Mandrell	Boris Yeltsin

4

DOUBLE BIRTH ORDERS

The One/Only

WHEN IS A ONE NOT A ONE?

ONE/ONLIES

This is not a question from a Chinese parable but a real problem in birth order interpretation. When I used the traditional birth orders to try to understand my patients, it didn't take long for me to realize that the behaviors I was expecting to see did not occur 100 percent of the time. Some of my first-born children were acting like onlies, and some of the second-borns were also showing some "only" characteristics. Third-borns, at times, were also acting like only children. Something was either very wrong with the birth order characteristics, or the whole concept was flawed. Looking at the situation more closely, I discovered that these patients had much older and younger brothers or sisters. This meant that each of these widely spaced children was being raised as a type of only child because of the large age gaps between siblings.

First-Born with Much Younger Sibling

It appeared that the magic number of years of separation was four, or, more important, four school years. With this interval, the children rarely interacted with their older or younger siblings or their friends. For a child, the four-year gap between a fourth grader and an eighth grader is enormous. I now had the concept of a *double birth order* for these children, and found that they had a unique set of characteristics when combined with their ordinal birth order.

THE DOUBLE BIRTH ORDER = ONE/ONLY

Now we will see when a one isn't necessarily a one. How do the characteristics of an only child combine with those of a first-born? This concept is so central to the *real understanding* of birth order that it must be described before the other birth orders.

The only child becomes a first-born when more siblings are added to the family. It is now that the spacing between the children becomes significant. If a second birth is *within* four years or, more specifically, four school years, this falls within the traditional ordinal system. The first-born is a one and the second-born a two.

If the second birth occurs more than four years after the first birth, a double birth order emerges. At a four-year spacing, the older child shows 50 percent "only" and 50 percent first-born characteristics. As the years increase between the first and second birth, the percentage of "only" characteristics increase and the first-born characteristics diminish. This can be shown as follows:

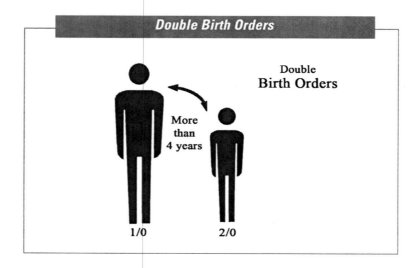

A. First-born (fewer than four years to) second-born. First-born loses most of the "only" characteristics and becomes a true first-born #1.

B. First-born (four years to) second-born. First-born is 50 percent only and 50 percent first-born. Is a #1/0.

C. First-born (six years to) second-born. First-born is 60 percent only and 40 percent first-born. This is where we start to get more only characteristics. This person can be a #1/0 or #0/1.

D. First-born (seven to eight years to) second-born. First-born is 70 to 80 percent only and 20 to 30 percent first-born. Is a #0/1.

E. First-born (twelve years to) second-born. First-born is 95 percent only and 5 percent first-born. Is a #0/1 and is much more like an only than a #1.

The designation only/one (#0/1) was not created to further confuse the issue. As the time between siblings increases, the first-born characteristics weaken and the "only" characteristics strengthen.

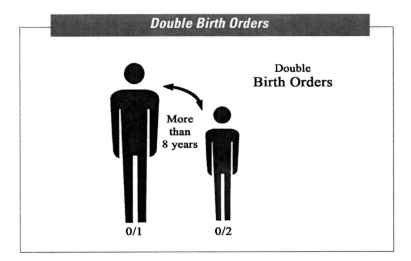

The term only/one (as seen in examples C, D, and E when the time between the children is six, eight, or twelve years) is a reflection of their true characteristics. These percentages are estimates at best, but I have witnessed them in my office over the past thirty-five years and the difference is real.

Let's look at the dynamics that take place in the first-born's family when the second-born is born four or more years afterward. The first-born is already in nursery school and about to go off to kindergarten. He has his own friends, so the new baby does not seem like much of a threat to his throne. As they grow older these years of separation keep them from close interaction. With other families where the years between the two births is greater than four years, the likelihood of competition for the throne is greatly diminished. The two children grow up in almost separate families. They have little in common, as they are at different levels of development both mentally and socially. They have their own friends and activities, and, usually, separate rooms.

With increased spacing between children, parents can give both children most of the benefits that an only would receive, both financial and emotional. How do these one/onlies act as children and adults? We might think of them as first-borns with a vitamin boost. If they are the "bossy" leaders, they are much stronger and can withstand more criticism than if they were a regular first-born. One/onlies don't share the respect for adults and authority figures that the first-borns have and can be confrontational to both peers and parents. You might say the addition of the only characteristics adds power to the first-born and lets him really take charge.

The one/only is not trapped in the adult world and the older generation. He does not feel alone like an only child, but can easily swing back and forth between the adult world and the child world. This ability to be "generational," so to speak, is a unique characteristic of the one/only. They appear to need to be in positions of power to satisfy their desire to lead. They are so strong that the adult rules so important to the first-born are not much of a damper on their behavior.

I've noticed that the gender of the one/only is important. If it's a boy, he is especially close to his mother and wants to be strong and conquer his fears. If it's a girl, she's closer to her father and, as is so true with only children, will emulate his behavior. If the child is the more quiet and introspective one/only, the combination can make for a very quiet, introspective person. This person will indeed possess a lot of power and self-confidence; it's just not readily apparent. Some examples of people we all know will help to clarify the one/only personality.

Life Stories

Ron (Willie) Howard, the actor and director, was born in 1954, and his brother, Clinton, was born five years later, in 1959. Ron got an early start in show business as little red-haired Opie on the *Andy Griffith Show*. Very

What's His Name?

This one/only has a sister, Kathy, five years younger. He said the separation amounted to light years between them; "as children we were in separate universes." He is brutally honest and gets right to the point, but is still a charmer. He did a lot of fighting as a kid and lost most of his fights. He just didn't want to submit to the fear he had of fighting. After one loss he went to the other boy's house and complained to his father that he was beaten up. This is something only a one/only would do. Talking to adults is no problem. He would later go on to have a very successful television talk show. We are talking about Phil Donahue. His second wife, actress Marlo Thomas, is an only/one (ten years older than her brother Tony), demonstrating the tendency of like birth orders to be attracted to each other.

early in his career, he became a film director and was quite successful—a one/only isn't afraid to take a chance and go it alone. In his case, directing others came naturally, a first-born trait. His brother Clinton starred in the *Gentle Ben* series, but has not achieved the fame of his older brother. Ron would have been a tough act to follow, so some sibling rivalry may take place even when the spacing between siblings is five years.

Ron Howard

Clinton recalled that when the boys were younger Ron wanted to enter a film contest and needed his brother to act in his home movie. Clinton made Ron sign a contract for part of the profits if he won the contest. Ron did win, but was reluctant to hand over the money. As Clinton recalls, their father had to step in to help enforce the contract.

Madeleine Korbel Albright, secretary of state under Bill Clinton, was born in 1937. Her next younger sibling, Kathy, was born in 1942, five years later. As the first female secretary of state, Madeleine had no fear of taking on the leaders of the Middle East, even though their attitudes toward women in power were somewhat negative.

Actress and comedian Lucille Ball, born in 1911, had a younger brother, Fred, born in 1915. Lucy blazed a trail in comedy for women. She was one of the first women to produce her own show and control its direction.

Newt Gingrich, the former Speaker of the House, is a one/only. He has four younger half-sisters he grew up with after his mother remarried. His career has certainly been filled with controversy that he has weathered very well. Newt is especially close to his mother—can anyone forget Connie Chung's interview with her? His mother was as outspoken as her son.

President George W. Bush is now a one/only, but was originally a first-born, with a sister three years younger. The space between siblings increased to seven years after his younger sister died of leukemia at three years old. George was then seven years old. He and his brother, Jeb, the former governor of Florida, are seven years apart. After his sister's death, George started taking on one/only characteristics, being more sensitive to his mother's feelings. His uncle is said to have noticed that he expressed adult emotions about the death of his sister. He has shown this one/only strength in his ability to confront his critics of the Iraq war policy and withstand negative criticism.

The characteristics of the only/ones, those with eight years or more between siblings, show even greater "only" characteristics.

Woody Allen (Allan Stewart Konigsberg), actor, director, and screen-writer, was born in 1935 and has a sister, Letty Aronson, eight years younger. He can be considered as an only/one. His life as a film director has been filled with wonderful individual creativity, as well as control of others. He has also weathered criticism of his bizarre personal behavior.

Former president Bill Clinton is another example of an only/one, as his half-brother, Roger, is ten years younger. Bill's connection with his mother was exceptionally close. It may have been that she relied on him as the only male figure in the family between her divorces. We're all familiar with the controversy about Bill's social life. He resisted impeachment proceedings and lied to the grand jury. If this doesn't show the strength and self-assurance of the only/one, nothing else does. Here is an ironic twist: Monica Lewinsky, former White House intern, is a one/only born in 1973, followed by her brother, Michael, born in 1977. Her parents said they spaced the children four years apart so there would be no sibling rivalry—and they

Bill Clinton   Monica Lewinsky

were right! She and Clinton have similar birth orders, but he was more powerful as an only/one with ten years between siblings.

On a more somber note, Ted Bundy, the confessed serial killer, was at least five years older than his four stepsiblings by his mother's second husband. He didn't know until high school that this man was not his real father. Ted was a superb manipulator, became involved in politics, and even earned a Ph.D.

Another only/one who shows the quiet and withdrawn type is Ted Kaczynski, the Unabomber. He used his power for antisocial endeavors. In his mind, he was a crusader for social change. It was his brother, David, eight years younger, who turned him in to authorities.

FINAL THOUGHTS ON THE ONE/ONLY #1/0

Check to see how many years separate the first-born and the next sibling. Four school years make this first-born a one/only. The larger the distance between siblings, the more the first-born shows "only" characteristics. This person is very strong and lives in the world of adults like an only child, but he understands his own generation as well.

FINAL THOUGHTS ON THE ONLY/ONE #0/1

This child has many more than four years between him and a younger sibling (as much as eight years or more). This child can become almost a "second parent" to the younger sibling. He lives life as an only but can "feel" the presence of his younger sibling.

One/Onlies and Only/Ones					
Lucille Ball	4yr	1/0	Oprah Winfrey	6yr	1/0
Sydney Chaplin	4yr	1/0	Janis Joplin	6yr	1/0
Queen Elizabeth	4yr	1/0	Winston Churchill	6yr	1/0
Melissa Joan Hart	4yr	1/0	Elizabeth Montgomery	6yr	1/0
Mick Jagger	4yr	1/0	Dick Van Patten	6yr	1/0
Monica Lewinsky	4yr	1/0	Dick Van Dyke	6yr	1/0
David Nelson	4yr	1/0	Julia Louis-Dreyfus	6yr	1/0
Sylvester Stallone	4yr	1/0	Barack Obama	6yr	1/0
Leonard Bernstein	5yr	1/0	Sean Connery	8yr	0/1
Judge Judy Sheindlin	5yr	1/0	Woody Allen	8yr	0/1
Peter Frampton	5yr	1/0	Ted Kaczynski	8yr	0/1
Jimmy Swaggart	5yr	1/0	Andrew Carnegie	8yr	0/1
Billie Jean King	5yr	1/0	Sidney Sheldon	8yr	0/1
Maureen Reagan	5yr	1/0			
Madeleine Albright	5yr	1/0	Beau Bridges	8yr	0/1
Ted Bundy	5yr	1/0	Sandra Day O'Connor	8yr	0/1
Ron Howard	5yr	1/0	Bill Clinton	10yr	0/1
Phil Donahue	5yr	1/0	Marlo Thomas	10yr	0/1
Jon Bon Jovi	5yr	1/0	Alice B. Toklas	10yr	0/1
John Wayne	5yr	1/0	Mr. Fred Rogers	11yr	0/1
Daisy Fuentes	5yr	1/0	Carol Burnett	11yr	0/1
			Diahann Carroll	14yr+	0/1
			Mikhail Gorbachev	16yr	0/1
			Walter Mondale	24yr	0/1

5

DON'T TELL ME WHAT TO DO

The Second-Born

I'LL DO IT IF I WANT TO

The second child comes into the world with an older brother or sister and often two parents with whom to interact. Everyone is telling him what to do, and he doesn't like it. He wants to make a special place for himself in the family, and being stubborn gets him some attention. He is so strong-willed that even if he knows he's wrong, he will not give in.

Second-Born Characteristics
▪ Wants to control their own space
▪ Does not want to be told what to do
▪ Usually a better athlete than #1
▪ Outgoing personality
▪ Very competitive
▪ Can be a rebel

A glance at the family photo album can be very revealing. You are not going to see as many pictures of number two as you see of number one. Guess who else is in most of number two's photos? You guessed right: number one!

It's not so easy to talk about the number-two child without getting into all the variations. The first variation occurs when there are only two children in

Family photo album

the family. The second variation is seen when there are three children in the family; the second becomes the middle child. The problem with describing the second-born is that the gender of the older and younger siblings have a great impact on this position, depending on the gender of the second child. The following are the possible variations with two children in the family.

No matter how many children are in the family, the second child—like all children—wants to be special in his unique way. This child has his own

---

Variation #1

Variation #1: Two children in the family with fewer than four school years apart give us four possibilities.

	1A	1B	1C	1D
#1	Boy	Girl	Boy	Girl
#2	Boy	Girl	Girl	Boy

Variation #2

Variation #2: Three children in the family fewer than four school years apart give us eight possible combinations.

	2A	2B	2C	2D	2E	2F	2G	2H
#1	Boy	Girl	Boy	Boy	Girl	Girl	Boy	Girl
#2	Boy	Girl	Girl	Girl	Boy	Boy	Boy	Girl
#3	Boy	Girl	Girl	Boy	Boy	Girl	Girl	Boy

---

set of characteristics and strategies to make a place for himself. He especially wants to move up in birth order and take the throne away from his older brother or sister.

This child can be the most competitive of all the birth orders in his attempt to move up in the birth order ranking and "dethrone" number one. If he decides not to compete, he can chart a course in life so divergent from number one that he is in no obvious way competing for the number-one position. However, the competition is always there.

Let's look at the world through the eyes of the second-born. The second-born knows early in life that he has three choices: he must make his own way in the world, dethrone the first-born, or silently drop out. There is no second chance to make a good impression with these children; they are the masters at sizing up both you and the situation. They can spot a phony or insincere person right away.

When talking to parents of a second-born, I touch a nerve when I tell them that this child likes to make his own decisions, and more important, wants to know what's going to happen to him. The parents usually say, "That's my boy, how did you know?" They know you have your hands full with this child, and now realize that you understand their "stubborn" number two. Now you have their confidence.

The second child isn't stubborn; he just wants a little control over his life. Can you blame him? He has parents and an older sibling telling him what to do. Older children love feeding the younger ones misinformation on occasion, which leaves number two a little more wary and less trusting. The younger children who are reading this can likely remember lots of stories—tales of creatures under the bed, in the lake, and the like—fed to them by their older siblings.

To make themselves different from the first-born, second-borns are usually better athletes, since the older child has a head start in school. Even one year in school is a lot to overcome. However, should the first-born have trouble in school, you can bet the second-born will be getting straight As.

As a child and as an adult the second-born can have a warm, outgoing personality. He has had to develop better communication skills than his older sibling, and has a better ability to read people than the first-born.

Have you ever found yourself in a situation where the other person won't even enter into the conversation, and it seems one-sided? You may be in a conversation with a second-born who is trying to size up the situation, making you uncomfortable by being silent. This is the same trick they pulled on their older sibling.

Earlier, I gave you the words that many languages have for the first-born child. The second-born isn't that lucky—a special word for them doesn't always exist. One exception is Japan, where the name for the second child is *hiyameshi*, a word also meaning "cold rice." This is what the second-born gets after the first-born eats the warm rice with his parents. (Talk about creating low self-esteem!)

Sibling rivalry is an important component of how these children develop. The sexes of the first- and second-borns play a very important role in their behaviors. We will explore the twelve variations of the second-born position (in families with two and three children) and give examples to show how gender plays a part in the personality development.

SECOND-BORN BOY WITH OLDER BROTHER

There can be a lot of competition with this combination, especially if the second brother gets physically bigger than his older brother. There can be a switch in the birth orders if the older brother takes a nurturing role and does not want to compete. If the competition with the older brother is too tough, the second-born will chart a different course altogether or drop out completely.

Life Stories

Former president Ronald Reagan shows the classic switch in birth order. Ronald was the second of two boys; his brother, Neil, was two years older. Ron got bigger and stronger and became a better athlete and student then Neil. Ron became his brother's protector and even helped him get into college.

Reagan was called the "Great Communicator." This communication skill of second-borns is a two-way street, for as warm and friendly as they can be, they can also be cold, silent, and unfriendly, if threatened. (Caution—Don't Tread on Me!) It was said of Reagan that when everyone was going left-wing he was going right. It's always easier to hold your viewpoint when everyone around you agrees. He was almost always alone in his views, and had the strength of the second-born not to give in.

Actor Paul Newman had a brother one year older, Arthur Jr., named for his dad. This gives the number-one son

Ronald Reagan

another big edge in the game. Their father was an accountant and the owner of a sporting goods store in Cleveland. Arthur Jr. was a better student and athlete than Paul and followed his father into the family business. As athletic as Paul was, it's hard to believe he couldn't compete with his brother. (In college Paul was thrown off the football team for drunken brawling, and he says he graduated "magna cum lager.") Paul took a completely different course than his brother, and, typical of a number two,

Paul Newman

had enough money to control his life. With his many projects at a late age, he said, "I keep trying to retire from everything, and I discover I've retired from absolutely nothing." Number twos always seem to have a project or two in progress. One of Paul's greatest regrets was that his father died before he could see Paul as a success in the acting world.

Second-borns have a very keen sense of injustice, as they see their world in comparison to their older sibling and are always trying to "measure" up to number one. As an adult, money becomes very important, not in itself, but in its ability to give the number two independence. These are the eager beavers of birth order. As adults they always have a number of ongoing "projects," something they learned early in life.

Jesse Ventura, former wrestler and former governor of Minnesota, has a brother, Jan, three years older. Jesse brought a very different style to the governor's mansion. His no-nonsense, straight-shooter style was refreshing to many. We know about Jesse's wrestling career before he went into politics, but is politics really very different from wrestling?

Movies

To illustrate the two-boy combination we need to recall the 1992 movie *A River Runs Through It*. This was a story about two brothers growing up in Montana and finding their identities. They show the characteristics of the first and second-borns in a real-life setting. The father, a rigid Presbyterian minister, makes the second son, Paul, stay at the table until he finishes his dinner, which he doesn't want to do. In the morning, when everyone comes to the table for breakfast, Paul is still sitting at the table,

What's Her Name?

Her older brother's name is Paul. Their father was a pianist who left their mother for their best friend's mother when she was eight years old. She started training as a dancer and won a number of local contests. The week before she was to go to California on a dancing scholarship, the car she was riding in was hit by a train. She was thirteen years old and her leg was injured. The doctors said she would never dance again. It was during her convalescence, while listening to the radio, that she began to sing. She had natural talent and began singing with Les Brown's band when she was sixteen years old. One of her most famous songs was *Sentimental Journey*. Known as the "girl next door," she had a long movie career. Everything she did was perfect. Unpredictable and spontaneous, she is Mary Ann Kataloff— known to us as Doris Day.

his dinner untouched. This is typical behavior of a second-born: when he feels the need to control his life, he never gives in. The older brother, Norman, went east for a traditional college education while younger brother Paul stayed home to follow a different lifestyle, standing up for injustice as a newspaper reporter. Running through the movie was the theme of the river and fly-fishing. The father taught his sons the "Presbyterian style," to cast on a four-count rhythm between ten o'clock and two o'clock. As is typical of the second child, Paul broke free of this style and developed a casting rhythm all his own.

SECOND-BORN GIRL WITH OLDER SISTER

Rivalry is not as obvious between girls as it is between boys. Of course they sometimes fight, but in a more subtle way. The more athletic younger sister can become the cheerleader with the radiant personality while her older sister excels in the classroom. Because these children want to be different from each other, they may start to dress differently, join different clubs at school, and run with a completely different crowd of friends. Which sister takes the more "unusual" path? Usually the one who loses the sibling competition. If neither gives in, you may see two very similar girls.

Life Stories

Margaret Jane Pauley's sister was two grades ahead of her in school.[1] Painfully shy, Jane Pauley spent her entire second-grade year being called

Margaret and not Jane because she was too shy to correct the teacher. She said her life changed when she did not make the cheerleading squad in the tenth grade. She instead followed her sister's lead and joined the debate and public speaking team. After college and brief exposure to television news in Indianapolis and Chicago, she was offered a job on the *Today Show* in New York. No one could understand how she moved up so fast in the super competitive profession while she herself was so unaggressive. Perhaps Jane was playing her birth order as support person to her own two co-anchors, Tom Brokaw and Bryant Gumbel.

OLDER BOY/YOUNGER GIRL

This combination gives the brother the edge from the start, if he lives in a traditional family where the father is the primary breadwinner. In today's society, this is changing, and if the mother takes the dominant role in the family, the daughter would bond with dad and the older brother with mom. This could cause a little confusion.

Typically, the younger sister has three choices. First, she can compete with her brother academically. Second, she can compete athletically, becoming a "tomboy." Third, she can play the sex card and become the precious little princess, to get daddy's attention away from big brother.

Being the first girl, she has a special place in the family and may use it to her advantage. If a younger sister does dethrone an older brother, she is either a very high achiever or there has been a cultural switch in the family. The family may be matriarchal and run by mom. Here are some examples of high-achieving second-born women.

Life Stories

Actress Elizabeth Taylor has a brother, Howard, three years older. It's obvious she has taken on the role of the beautiful little girl. As we have followed her career, we have heard the stories of just how difficult and stubborn she can be. She is not afraid to stand up for the underdog, and she was an early supporter of efforts on behalf of AIDS research. She supported her friend Michael Jackson during his tough times, unafraid of the publicity and how it would reflect on her.

---

[1]Jane is technically a third-born child, but was raised as a functional second-born because her older brother died at birth.

THREE CHILDREN/SECOND-BORN GIRL WITH OLDER BROTHER AND YOUNGER BROTHER

This is much like the situation we just described, only we add a younger brother. Now the number-two child is truly in the middle but, as the only girl in the family, she has a chance to shine. Now she has four choices: compete academically, compete athletically, be the feminine little girl, or be the big sister to her little brother.

Life Stories

Martha Stewart, the homemaker diva, is in the middle between her older brother, Eric, who is two years older, and a younger brother, Frank. Her obsessive attention to detail is legendary. She has made a place for herself in a man's world, earning billions. She had a very nurturing relationship

Martha Stewart

with her father, who helped her even decorate for her senior prom. He encouraged her to excel. She is seen as a whirlwind of activity, always with a project. Money has always been important to her, as she has worked both as a model and in the brokerage houses on Wall Street. Her trial and conviction for insider stock trading and lying to the government led to a prison term for Martha. She agreed to serve her sentence while her appeal was pending. Many feel that she wasn't treated fairly and the "boys" just wanted to get back at her for being so successful in a man's world.

OLDER SISTER/YOUNGER BROTHER

This can be the most competitive combination between the first two children in a traditional family. By traditional I mean that the father takes the dominant role and the mother the secondary role. Why is this combination so competitive? We know that the second child has an inner urge to dethrone number one, and it's easier to do that if you're the first male child. The older sister has to be an overachiever just to keep her position.

As I said in the chapter on first-borns, when the second child is a male, his sister has a lot to overcome. It's even more difficult for the first-born girl to maintain her position when the boy is named after his father. If roles are reversed in the family and the mother is the dominant figure, then the older girl has an easier time keeping her position. This competition for power makes for some very interesting high-achievers in the world. The older sister can hold on to the number-one position and defeat her younger brother, or the younger brother can defeat his older sister.

Life Stories

Hillary Clinton, our former First Lady and now senator from New York, is the older child who kept her position even when her younger brother, Hugh, became an attorney like herself. We all have a sense of her power and her ability to use it. There was a story at the end of the Clinton administration that had Hugh trying to get some presidential pardons for profit. It looks like this number two has stopped competing with his sister.

Abraham Lincoln, our sixteenth president, had a sister, Sara, two years older. Much has been written about Lincoln, and his nickname, "Honest Abe," was only one indication of his character. His ability to keep the Union together during the Civil War has been the subject of many books. He made many difficult decisions in the face of much adversity and negative public opinion.

Jerry Seinfeld

Jerry Seinfeld, one of the highest-paid comedians, has a sister, Carolyn, eighteen months older. We know how well he has done financially. True to the nature of a second child, Jerry always has to have "projects." Since he left his television show, he got married and has started raising a family, has written a children's book, and is still traveling, doing stand-up comedy.

One of the most famous younger brothers was John Kennedy Jr. His sister, Caroline, was two years older. He was on his way to the number-one position with little opposition from her when his tragic plane accident ended his life.

THREE CHILDREN/SECOND BOY WITH OLDER BROTHER AND YOUNGER SISTER

This number two is truly a middle child. He has the greatest problem with his identity and making himself special. He is not the first boy, and the third child is the first girl. The competitive instincts of this number-two boy are moved into high gear with the birth of his sister, putting him truly in the middle. These are very special boys, and when focused, they go out of their way to be noticed and are not easily forgotten.

Life Stories

Former president George Herbert Walker Bush, born in 1924, has an older brother, Prescott Jr., born in 1922. George is sandwiched between Prescott and younger sister Nancy. Shortly after George began his family with his wife, Barbara, he left the family home in the East and made a complete break with family tradition. They made a new life in the Texas oil fields. George was out to find his fortune, leaving the East for the West. Later in his career he went into politics, becoming president of the United States; a goal of many but one attained by only a few.

Fashion designer Giorgio Armani was born in 1942, the second of three children. He had an older brother, Sergio, and a younger sister, Rosanna. He in no way competed with his older brother, but carved out a special spot for himself in the fashion world.

Another fashion designer, Roy Halston, was born in 1932, also the second of three children. He had an older brother, Bob, and a younger sister, Sue. He developed the "all-American chic" style and set himself apart from the other designers. He was a perfectionist and made millions—the security that a number two needs so others will not tell him what to do.

THREE CHILDREN/SECOND GIRL WITH OLDER SISTER AND YOUNGER BROTHER

I could find few examples of this family combination. This girl may not feel the need to compete until her little brother comes on the scene. She can go the athletic route if her older sister is into academics. She can compete athletically with her younger brother, and that would give her a special place in the family as the girl jock. With the addition of her little brother, the first boy, she does not want to be moved down into the third position.

Actress Cheryl Ladd is the younger of two girls with a younger brother. She is known as a very complex person and as a child was a tomboy, the athletic number two. She replaced Farrah Fawcett as a regular on the television show *Charlie's Angels*.

Another actress who shares this same birth order and family sibling arrangement is Marg Helgenberger, who plays a tough woman on the TV crime series *CSI*. She is very touchy about her first name and not shy to correct anyone who calls her Marge—she even did it at an awards presentation! She played a cancer victim in the film *Erin Brockovich*, showing her strength as an actress and playing a strong woman just like herself.

THREE CHILDREN/SECOND BOY WITH OLDER SISTER AND YOUNGER SISTER

This is another situation where we have a true middle child. This time he is special because he is the only boy in the family. If things go well for him, he can certainly compete athletically with the two girls and play his card as the only boy and protector to his sisters. He can also just ignore them and go his own way, pretending they are no competition at all.

Life Stories

Bill Gates, former CEO of Microsoft, and Warren Buffett, CEO of Berkshire Hathaway, are two of the richest men in the world. Both have older sisters. Bill's sister Kristi is one year older and is his tax accountant. His younger sister is nine years his junior. This is outside our four-year limit, but he is such a good example of a number two using money to control his life that I just had to include him. Gates is one of very few people who have gone to court against the federal government and was not afraid of the attorneys' fees.

Warren Buffett also has two sisters, one two years older and the other three years younger. Warren is called the Oracle of Omaha because of his success in picking just the right stocks. He refused to buy into the computer investing bubble and was proven right when the bubble burst—another example of the independence of the number two. Warren announced in 2006 that he is giving the bulk of his fortune to the Bill and Melinda Gates Foundation. Here again, like birth orders tend to work well together.

THREE CHILDREN/SECOND BOY WITH OLDER SISTER AND YOUNGER BROTHER

These second children are in that very tough sibling position where the boy tries to dethrone the older sister. The twist here is that he has a younger brother, so it can be two against one, and the parents may come to her rescue from her brothers. Typically, this boy has an edge to move up, since he is the first-born boy. His sister may just let him do it.

Life Stories

Bob Dole, former senator and presidential candidate, has this family order. His sister is two years older and his brother is two years younger. His life was built around his athletic abilities, and he played football, ran track, and played baseball. His injury in World War II almost cost him his life, but even with his disability this number two made it back and in control of his own destiny. He is known as a man of strong beliefs who sticks to them. He also possesses a great sense of humor, shown in his book on presidential wit and in his television commercials for Viagra and Pepsi.

Martin Luther King Jr. was a number two, with a sister two years older and a brother one year younger. His life showed the strength of the number two to challenge the civil rights system and keep up his indefatigable strength for his cause. He was that stubborn number two who just wouldn't give up.

THREE CHILDREN/SECOND GIRL WITH OLDER BROTHER AND YOUNGER SISTER

This position makes this second child the first girl in the family. Like any younger sister with an older brother, she can try to compete any way she can. The older brother can be very supportive of his younger sisters and not see them as a threat. If this happens, this number two can use her position as the older of two girls and mother her younger sister and try to ignore her older brother.

Kathie Lee Gifford, actress, singer, and talk-show hostess, has certainly done it her way. She is the second child and has an older brother, Davy, whom she called Day-Day. She says that since he didn't have any brothers, he made his sisters into tomboys to play with him. Davy is now a minister. Kathie wears both the athlete and academic hats very well. Her communication skills are hard to deny, as seen on her former television show *Live with Regis and Kathie Lee*. It looks like she can do it all, and I think she dethroned her brother.

THREE CHILDREN/SECOND GIRL WITH OLDER SISTER AND YOUNGER SISTER

In this family of girls, no one is special because of their gender, so everyone is on her own to be different. We don't see a lot of outward physical confrontations with the girls, but they can certainly be students, athletes, and artists. Let's take a look at a few families that show this arrangement.

Life Stories

Peggy Fleming, a world champion ice skater, has a sister one year older and one a year younger. It was said that she looked like her dad and grew up a tomboy. She has been described as a little removed and a bit cool, but extremely funny and loving. Her mom was also a tomboy and was very supportive of her skating. Peggy resisted her domineering and controlling mother. Once, when her mother felt she needed to gain weight and forced her to eat a steak, Peggy just went to the bathroom and spit it out. As always, never try to tell a number two what to do.

Eva Braun, Hitler's mistress, was the second of a three-girl family. All the girls were three years apart. Eva was an athletic girl and can be seen swimming and doing exercises in some of their home movies. As a teenager she was quite rebellious. Her life with Hitler may have had its origin in her relationship with her father—he had both political and moral objections to their relationship. Hitler set her up in an apartment, paid for everything, and let her have a carefree life. She seems to have ignored what was happening in Germany during World War II. As long as she had everything she wanted, she didn't care. Braun and Hitler took their lives in the *Führerbunker* when Russia's Red Army entered Berlin.

THREE CHILDREN/SECOND BOY WITH OLDER BROTHER AND YOUNGER BROTHER

This last family arrangement is all boys. If everyone is into athletics, they better each pick a different sport. Three boys have the same ways to compete as girls: academically, athletically, and artistically. Each child can choose something different or compete head-on. With three boys, the testosterone level will definitely be high.

A great example of this kind of family is Mark McGuire, the baseball player who broke Babe Ruth's home-run record. All of his brothers were athletes, but Mark was the most outstanding and went to the head of the pack.

FINAL THOUGHTS ON THE SECOND-BORN #2

When assessing a second-born, look to see who is above and below him in birth order in the family with three children. Gender does make a difference, so check this out as well. Look to see if this second-born has dethroned his older sibling, being better both athletically and academically. He may also have used his gender to win favor with the dominant parent. Conversely, has this second-born been thoroughly defeated by the older sibling and dropped out?

Second-borns can have both an outgoing personality and a very quiet side when they feel uncertain in a difficult situation. This is the birth order that has difficultly admitting they are wrong. Never ever tell the second-born what to do. Let it be their decision.

Who said understanding birth order was easy? With twelve types of number twos, you can zero in on their true personalities and what makes them so special. Who has the last word but that famous number two Jacob Cohen, also known as Rodney Dangerfield. He had an older sister, Marion, who his mother pushed into acting. His parents divorced when he was ten and his father, who was in vaudeville, saw the family only one or two times a year. Rodney, a number two, used his position and his self-deprecating humor to tell it all: "I just don't get no respect."

Second-Borns

Princess Anne	Kathie Lee Gifford	Rupert Murdock
Abel	Bryant Gumbel	Ozzie Nelson
John Quincy Adams	Alexander Hamilton	Paul Newman
Giorgio Armani	Prince Harry	Wayne Newton
Fred Astaire	Marg Helgenberger	Annie Oakley
Joan Baez	Patrick Henry	Jane Pauley
Warren Beatty	Benny Hill	Ronald Reagan
John Belushi	Nicky Hilton	Cal Ripken Jr.
Eva Braun	Lee Iacocca	Norman Rockwell
Warren Buffett	Catherine Zeta-Jones	Diana Ross
George H. W. Bush	John Kennedy Jr.	Donald Rumsfeld
Johnny Carson	John Kerry	Kurt Russell
David Crosby	Martin Luther King Jr.	Arnold Schwarzenegger
Jamie Lee Curtis	Calvin Klein	Jerry Seinfeld
Billy Ray Cyrus	Cheryl Ladd	Tom Selleck
Rodney Dangerfield	Michael Landon	Dr. Seuss
Doris Day	Abraham Lincoln	Dinah Shore
Cameron Diaz	John Walker Lindh	Dick Smothers
Angie Dickinson	Greg Louganis	George Stephanopoulos
Bob Dole	Lee Marvin	Martha Stewart
Sarah Ferguson	John McCain	Elizabeth Taylor
Peggy Fleming	Mark McGuire	Jessie Ventura
Redd Foxx	Jenny McCarthy	Robert J. Wagner
Roy Halston Frowick	Timothy McVeigh	Tennessee Williams
Bill Gates	Robert Mitchum	

6

THE PRINCE AND PRINCESS OF BIRTH ORDER

The Two/Only

THE TWO/ONLY #2/0

When four or more years separate the first two children, the second child has two birth orders: that of a second-born and that of an only child. The separation between the children allows the parents to give this child almost as much attention as they would give an only child. The two/only also has the personality characteristics of a second-born.

What does the addition of the only child nurturing do for the second-born? It adds power. Unlike the one/only, in which the birth orders share similar characteristics, the only and second-born do not. The addition of the only's self-assured characteristics and no fear of adults makes a "stubborn two" into an immovable object.

The addition of the only's characteristics converts or modifies the "good personality" of the second-born into a force to manipulate others for his own agenda. The second child wants to control his own space, and two/onlies are second to none at accomplishing this. This birth order can be one of the most powerful positions among birth orders. If they harness their power to benefit others, much can be accomplished.

In my practice I call these children my stealth patients. I'm never quite sure how I'm being manipulated by them or through their manipulation of their parents. The girls, when delicate in appearance, can fool you, as they have extremely high pain thresholds. They can break the "unbreakable" orthodontic appliances. These children can use their strong will and high pain thresholds to excel in sports or academics. It's mind over matter, and this birth order has the toughness of none other.

Just as we have seen with all the birth orders, there is a flip side. Two/onlies can use their power to manipulate others for their own use, acting like princes and princesses.

Some might ask if sibling rivalry enters into the equation. It does, but only slightly, since the four school years between the siblings seem to negate any real rivalry. To mom and dad a two/only is almost like an only child.

Does gender make a difference? A little, but then the distance between the children weakens any real effect. The first-born of each gender does have a "special" place with the parent of the opposite sex.

People with this birth order can be very high achievers and show little fear of authority or difficult situations throughout life.

Life Stories

Pop singer Britney Spears has a brother, Bryan, five years older, and a sis-

Britney Spears

ter, Jamie Lynn, ten years younger. Britney shows the power of the two/only to control her career. She shows the adult characteristics of the only as she makes her own way in the music field. At twenty-six years of age, she certainly can hold her own with others much older. In June 2002, Forbes magazine named her the "pop princess," and she was "crowned" the world's most powerful celebrity. This distinction was based on combined earnings and media exposure. Notice the choice of words: "princess" and "crowned." Britney has known her princess status all along; only now is the media catching on.

Much has happened in her life—good and bad—that has kept her center stage. Two marriages, two divorces, and two children.

Former secretary of state Colin Powell has a sister, Marilyn, who is five and a half years older. We all know the story of how a boy from the Bronx became the chairman of the Joint Chiefs of Staff in the first Bush administration and then secretary of state in the second. A reporter asked how he achieved all he had done in life when he barely made it through high school and was not a great student in college. Colin simply replied to the reporter, "Isn't America great?" If a two/only is going to let you into their world, it's going to be on their terms.

Barbra Streisand

Singer and actress Barbra Streisand, born in 1942, has an older brother, Sheldon Jay, born six years earlier. The role of princess is not a bad fit for Barbra. She has certainly been in control of her career, both in acting and music. Her mom said of her, "She was an excellent but troublesome student. She always saw everything depending on how it affected her." Definitely a two/only personality trait!

Actor and comedian Dudley Moore was nicknamed "Cuddly Dudley," but he manipulated women all his life. He had an older sister, Barbara, who was at least four years older. Some say his relationship with his mother and his birth defects (a shortened leg and club foot) influenced his personality. He certainly showed the strength to overcome many of his problems. Two/onlies come in all sorts of packages.

Princess Margaret Rose, whose sister, Queen Elizabeth, was four years older, died three days after the start of her sister's celebration of her fiftieth anniversary on the throne. Princess Margaret was the first divorcée in the royal family. She was a high-spirited, partygoing person—truly a princess's princess. A courtier who collided with her cartwheeling down a corridor as a child was reported to say, "Thank God the other one was born first!"

If control is a quality needed by a talk-show host, who better to run one than a two/only? David Letterman and Jay Leno share this birth order. David has a sister, Janice, who is four years older. David's move from one television

What's His Name?

His parents are Holocaust survivors. His older sister, Evelyn, was born in England in 1940. He was born in England in 1944. They came to America in 1949 and his father continued to work as a toy maker. They talked politics all the time, as his parents loved the freedom of speech in America. He went to Tulane University in New Orleans and saw the seedier side of life in the French Quarter. He graduated from Northwestern Law School and practiced law in Cincinnati. He ran for and won a seat on the Cincinnati city council. When the council found he had been visiting prostitutes (he paid with a check), he had to leave office in disgrace. He then started anchoring a news show and went on to win the mayor's race a few years later. He has a warm, outgoing, confident personality and is a real charmer. He now hosts a very popular talk show where almost anything goes. He is Jerry Springer.

network to another shows his desire to control his life and call the shots. Some celebrities won't appear on his show because of his dominating personality.

Jay Leno is a little different, because his brother is ten years older. Jay is an only/two, showing more "only" characteristics. If you have seen the two shows, you see Leno as less confrontational than Letterman, you might say, more respectful of his guests—more adult-like.

The unforgettable line "I am in control here" was spoken by a two/only, General Alexander Haig Jr., while secretary of state under President Ronald Reagan. He was not really the next in line to be in charge—he was fifth in the line of succession. Yet when Reagan was shot he stepped up to the plate and tried to take control. Alexander has a sister, Regina, four years older, an attorney, and a brother four years younger, a Jesuit priest.

Two/onlies are also represented on the negative side. David Duke, the former head of the Ku Klux Klan, has a sister, Dottie, five years older. David has stood up to the establishment for many years. He appears unflappable and unwilling to change his views. When on television interviews he almost never loses his temper and stays cool, often under a barrage of insults. Two/onlies can take it.

FINAL THOUGHTS ON THE TWO/ONLY #2/0

When looking at two/onlies, the years between the siblings are important. The strength of the two's traits are mellowed by the increase in years between siblings, giving them more "only" influence. These people are very controlling and manipulative of others—it's good if they are on your side. They expect to be treated like a prince or princess. Don't disappoint them.

Two/Onlies and Only/Twos					
Margaret Thatcher	4yr	2/0	David Duke	5yr	2/0
Jacques-Yves Cousteau	4yr	2/0	Michael Reagan	5yr	2/0
Armand Hammer	4yr	2/0	Britney Spears	5yr	2/0
David Letterman	4yr	2/0	Colin Powell	5yr	2/0
Cheryl Tiegs	4yr	2/0	Gilda Radner	5yr	2/0
Ben Stiller	4yr	2/0			
Princess Margaret-Rose	4yr	2/0	Barbra Streisand	6yr	2/0
General Alexander Haig Jr.	4yr	2/0	Burt Reynolds	6yr	2/0
Helen Gurley Brown	4yr	2/0	Maria Callas	6yr	2/0
Ted Danson III	4yr	2/0	Oona O'Neill Chaplin	6yr	2/0
Jerry Springer	4yr	2/0			
Ellen DeGeneres	4yr	2/0	Jaclyn Smith	7yr	0/2
Jesse James	4yr	2/0	Monica Seles	8yr	0/2
Charlie Chaplin Jr.	4yr	2/0	David Kaczynski	8yr	0/2
Calista Flockhart	4yr	2/0	Jeff Bridges	8yr	0/2
Ricky Nelson	4yr	2/0	Tom Clancy	8yr	0/2
Howard Stern	4yr	2/0	Neil Simon	9yr	0/2
Cybill Shepherd	4yr	2/0	Farrah Fawcett	9yr	0/2
Spencer Tracy	4yr	2/0	Gloria Steinem	9yr	0/2
Steve Martin	4yr	2/0	Al Gore	10yr	0/2
			Jay Leno	10yr	0/2
George Orwell	5yr	2/0	Lizzie Borden	10yr	0/2
Jerry Van Dyke	5yr	2/0	Spiro Agnew	11yr	0/2
George Carlin	5yr	2/0	Elizabeth Dole	13yr	0/2
Dustin Hoffman	5yr	2/0	John Dillinger	14yr	0/2

7

I FEEL YOUR PAIN

The Third-Born

THE THIRD-BORN #3

Third-borns can be the most sensitive and intuitive people. They see the world around them very differently than the other birth orders. What gives this child the special ability to understand the subtleties in people? When these children came into the world, they found a family with four people to understand. We are describing a true third-born, when there are fewer than four years between each of the three siblings. If we take a look at the family photo album we will find even fewer photos of this child than of number two—and yes, most pictures will be group photos of all the children, number three included.

Third-Born Characteristics
■ Very sensitive
■ Crying on the inside, laughing on the outside
■ Artistic and creative
■ Cares about others
■ Intuitive
■ Gentle, sweet
■ Playful

As we look at all the possible combinations of relationships, you can understand why the third-born is a master at working with groups of people.

There are numerous family relationships he must understand. First is the relationship between mom and dad, and next between his first and second siblings. The interrelationships between the first-born with mom, first-born with dad, second-born with mom, and then with dad are more complicated. (See Figure A on adjacent page.) Then the first and second children together with mom, and first and second together with dad. (See Figure B on adjacent page.) Last, the interrelationship of the third-born with all these people gives us at least fourteen different combinations. (See Figures C1, C2, and C3 on adjacent page.) It's confusing to those of us who are not third-borns, but it's all in a day's work for them.

Being so sensitive, third-borns truly "feel your pain." They see the world from a very different perspective than do first- and second-borns. They don't crave the power over others that the first-born does, nor do they want to control their own space like the second-born. They see the world differently and express themselves in artistic or humanitarian ways. In life, this birth order has more freedom to experience non-traditional aspects of society. Some may see them as weak and easily influenced by others. Instead, consider that it may just be their need to experience things on a more personal level. As with all the birth orders, there are two sides to the third-born.

Many have a very deep commitment to religion. Ruth Carter Stapleton, former president Jimmy Carter's younger sister, became an evangelist. Peter Boyle Jr., the actor who played the father in the sitcom *Everybody Loves Raymond* studied to become a Christian Brother. Mother Teresa made her life a commitment to religion as she helped the poor of India.

My experience with third-born patients is that they are truly more sensitive to pain than the other birth orders. This is the child whose Flintstones bandage stays on forever after he scrapes his knee. When being tested by older siblings, third-borns know that they can't let the older siblings see that they are hurting, or they will never stop getting picked on. If number two is fighting for a higher place, who better to vent frustration on than a younger sibling?

Many number threes show a very hard exterior to the world to protect their sensitive nature. This appearance of an impenetrable exterior is just a disguise.

I recall one of my patients, a 6'5", 300-pound mountain of a man, who told me that when receiving orthodontic treatment as a child he just had to take off his braces because they were too painful. I told him I under-

Third-Born Relationships

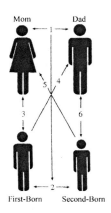

A

B

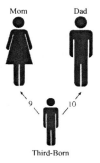

C1

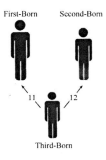

C2

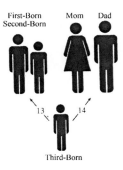

C3

stood that he was very sensitive to pain and would proceed with the lightest of force to straighten his teeth. (It seemed the right choice since he was easily twice my size.) We were successful with this gentle approach and did not have to remove his braces until we completed his treatment.

The statement "laughing on the outside, crying on the inside" would be appropriate for the third child. On the surface, they seem a lot tougher than they really are. However, when they just can't keep up the façade any longer, look out for a tidal wave of emotion. Third-borns can really experience a meltdown that reveals their emotional makeup. Helping others and working in the arts and other creative endeavors—especially ones in which they use their hands—are their natural tendencies. Remember the story of Ferdinand the bull? Ferdinand would rather smell the flowers than fight in the ring. That's the third child.

In the family third-borns may be thought of as dreamers or peacemakers. They sense the tensions in the family and want everything to be right. They are the masters of playing one sibling against the other. Of course mom and dad would never think that this little angel could be so devious. Third-borns are good at coming and going emotionally—their method of self-protection. Close one minute, distant the next....frustrating if you don't expect it.

What's Her Name?

She was born in Michigan in 1918 and has two older brothers, Bob and Billie. Her father was a traveling salesman and wasn't home very much. They found out later he had a drinking problem, but they never saw it around the house. He died tragically of carbon monoxide poisoning while working under their car. She was just sixteen years old. She had started dancing as a child and became quite good; she even went to New York City to train and dance professionally. She married an attorney from her hometown and found herself alone raising their sons when he went into politics. She found comfort in alcohol but later kicked the habit. She even founded an alcohol and drug rehabilitation hospital that is quite famous today. She received a Presidential Medal of Freedom for her work. Her maiden name was Elizabeth Ann Bloomer, now known as former first lady Betty Ford.

Gender Effect on the Third-Born

As in all birth orders, gender and position in the family make a difference. The third-born can have siblings of the same or different gender or one of each. I will address all the possible combinations and their gender effects.

Possible gender combinations in families with third-borns:

Third-Born Gender Combinations								
	3A	3B	3C	3D	3E	3F	3G	3H
#1	Boy	Girl	Boy	Girl	Girl	Boy	Girl	Boy
#2	Boy	Girl	Boy	Girl	Boy	Girl	Boy	Girl
#3	Boy	Girl	Girl	Boy	Girl	Boy	Boy	Girl

THIRD-BORN BOY WITH TWO OLDER BROTHERS

With three boys, the testosterone level within the family can really be high. The sibling rivalry between the first two boys can let number three escape and pursue his own course. This is because there are no special expectations on the third boy and the pressure is off. His direction could be very different from his two competitive brothers. He might choose not to participate in their affairs but will always be able to join in if he wants. If the normal sibling relationships are in order (i.e., sibling rivalry), then he can slip under the radar and become the sensitive, caring, emotional sponge for the world around him. He can watch the rivalry between his older siblings from a distance.

Life Stories

Comedic actor Leslie Nielsen is the third of three boys. Raised in the Northwest Territory of Canada, the son of a Mountie, Leslie was described as a very loveable kid. We really see his personality revealed in the *Naked Gun* movies as he plays the bumbling detective Frank Drebin.

Charlie Sheen had two older brothers but also a younger sister. He chose to compete athletically and was a very good pitcher in high school. He showed his unconventional side when he decided not to graduate from high school, and he became a rebel, experimenting with drugs. His life as we see it is still in turmoil but no one can dispute his acting abilities.

President Dwight Eisenhower was the third of six boys born into a Mennonite family. It's interesting that he went into the military, something not often seen among Mennonites. It was reported that he hated the hazing at West Point and suffered bouts of depression later in life. He took up painting on the advice of Winston Churchill and was a fly fisherman—and of course we all saw him on the golf course. All these activities allowed him to commune with nature and express his creativity and sensitivity.

Dwight Eisenhower

THIRD-BORN GIRL WITH TWO OLDER SISTERS

Things are a bit different here because the sibling rivalry isn't expressed among girls to the same extent as in a family of boys. It's there, just at a lower level. The third-born girl can slip under the radar, do her own thing, and not compete with her older siblings, or she can pick an area that she feels comfortable with and participate. Always remember the sensitivity of these little girls, as they are highly attuned to the world around them. To date I have found no examples of this birth order type in the media.

When I looked at the patients in my practice, I found several of these number three girls and I must say they didn't stand out in any particular way. We always remember the "special" children for what they say or do. These girls were just no trouble at all. Very polite, low-key, delightful patients. Maybe it's the lack of tension in a family of girls or the fact that they don't have to prove anything to make themselves special. They are allowed to express their sensitivity and do their own thing without interference.

THE THIRD-BORN, FIRST OF THEIR GENDER

The gender differences in a family that has three children make for a very confusing set of circumstances for the third-born. If the two older siblings are of the opposite sex (3C and 3D from chart on page 75), then the third child becomes the first-born boy or girl. Because of this, they are special in the family. If he is the first boy with two older sisters, he is forced to act stronger than may be natural for him. (You're the only boy, so be the man in the family!)

If she is the first girl with two older brothers, she can be the little princess protected by her older brothers, or she will be a tomboy to compete with them. For a third-born girl with two older brothers, her sweetness and sensitivity is in keeping with what is traditionally expected of her gender. Can she play the gender card to get what she wants? You bet, and if it works she keeps playing it all her life. If her parents become ill when she is an adult, she may be called upon by her brothers, as the only girl, to take the role as a number one and take charge of the situation. This new role is not a natural for her and she will find it very difficult.

THIRD-BORN GIRL WITH TWO OLDER BROTHERS

Life Stories

Singer and actress Madonna is an example of this birth order position. She has two older brothers, one and two years older. Their mother died when Madonna was five, so she became the lady of the house, but not for long. Her father quickly remarried and she had to share central billing with her stepmother. This third-born shows a tough exterior but also has the ability to transform herself in many ways. Her sensitivity at reading the public has kept her front and center for a long time. Her great interest and involvement in Kabbalah, a mystical interpretation of the Scriptures, is in keeping with her birth order.

Actress and former talk-show hostess Rosie O'Donnell had a similar childhood, with two older brothers and the loss of her mother when she was eleven. She assumed the role of mother in the house. As her father did not remarry, he and her brothers were her role models. She chose the tomboy façade, which she still shows today. We can all see this as the very tough outer shell she uses to protect herself. We know of her sensitive side, which she shows to all her adopted children. When she is not threatened, she is a very different person. I think a closer view of her life would reveal a softer nature, as the "hard shell" is just for protection.

Madonna

THIRD-BORN BOY WITH TWO OLDER SISTERS

If the third-born is a boy with two older sisters, he is usually encouraged by his father not to show his sensitive side. He must be tough and take on the male role like a number-one child. To him this is just an act, not anything that he really believes or understands. He may exaggerate this "dominant" male role, since it is just an act. I remember a situation in my office when the father of one of our patients refused to pay a bill. He insisted that the insurance company was responsible even though he had personally agreed to pay for the procedure. First he got indignant with the insurance company, then yelled and screamed at my office staff with some of the most profane language I have ever heard. His behavior was way out of line for an eighty-dollar charge. I finally got him into the office and talked with him. He was a third-born with two older sisters. His wife was a first-born and handled all the financial dealings, but she was in the hospital recovering from cancer surgery. He apologized for his behavior, pulled out his checkbook, paid the eighty dollars, and smiled, becoming the nice number three again.

Life Stories

Actor Marlon Brando Jr. had two older sisters. Jocelyn was five years older and Frances was two years older. His life could be the script for a third-born

Marlon Brando

with two older sisters. Growing up, Marlon demonstrated explosive emotions, always taking up for the underdog (the sensitive three trait). Later in life he would not accept his Academy Award for his role in *The Godfather*, but sent Sacheen Littlefeather, an Indian activist, to protest the way Native Americans were treated by the movie studios. Marlon's father was a bully and said he wouldn't amount to anything. This may have been his way of trying to make his son more like a number-one child, since he was the first boy. His parents separated when he was eleven and Marlon became the "man" of the house, a role for which he was not naturally suited. This was the same time he met Wally Cox, the actor who played Robinson Peepers on *Mister Peepers* television series.

He connected with Cox at age eleven, later became his roommate, and lifetime friend. When Cox died at age forty-eight Marlon took his ashes away from his wife and kept them under his bed for the rest of his life. Wally Cox's wife said, "Marlon needs them more than me." When he died both their ashes were cast in the waters off his Tahitian island. The movie roles he took show him as a very strong person, though deep inside he was more sensitive than strong. He had eleven children, five with his three wives, three with his housekeeper, and three from affairs. It was said he just loved the romance. Addicted to food, he once weighed over three hundred pounds and said it was a better addiction than alcohol.

What's His Name?

He is the third of three boys and played in a rock band in high school. Because of his size (over 6'6"), the wrestling coach said he should join the team. He was very reserved and even shy, which he covered up with attitude. He was known as the Mellow Giant, a teddy bear and very laid-back. He became a professional wrestler, rising to the top, and has also done some acting. His trademark is the American flag and his blond hair. He was born Terry Bollea but you know him as Hulk Hogan.

Norman Schwarzkopf, the U.S. Army general who was in charge of Operation Desert Storm, is a first-born son, with two older sisters: Anne, four years older, and Sally, two years older. His father took him to the Middle East as a teenager because he felt that all the women in the family were affecting Norman's masculinity. While General Schwarzkopf was in command, he showed compassion for his troops. He was a general who could understand their pain.

Jack Palance, an actor with a very macho persona, had two older sisters. He was the first-born son and became a good athlete in school. After college he was a boxer: how's that for taking on the role of first-born protector? His movie roles also exhibited a tough character. I wonder how many people know he was also a novelist, painter, and poet?

THIRD-BORN GIRL WITH SECOND-BORN BROTHER AND FIRST-BORN SISTER

With this combination, the third-born girl can again stay under the radar and let the two older siblings fight it out for the number-one position.

There is always a lot of rivalry between the second-born boy and first-born girl. This tension may affect the third-born if the confrontation gets tough and she sees herself as the peacemaker. She can also be the instigator, as she can read the relationships very well.

Life Stories

Third-borns have different priorities and see life differently than the other birth orders. Mother Teresa, a nun known for her unselfish service to the poor in India, had an older sister and an older brother. Her father died when she was eight years old, and her mother, though destitute, still helped others. The example of her mother's kindness was not lost on Mother Teresa.

Grace Patricia Kelly, the Hollywood princess, married Prince Rainier of Monaco. Her older siblings were all very athletic, but Grace was a sickly child. Her father was a former Olympian, so Grace was really out of the running for her dad's attention. It was said that she lived in her own dream world, aloof and cold on the outside but very vulnerable inside. Her world was a fairy tale, after all. She did three films with Alfred Hitchcock: *Dial M for Murder*, *Rear Window*, and *To Catch a Thief*. Her death in a car accident in Monaco was a tragic end to a beautiful life.

Barbara Pierce Bush, wife of one president and mother of another, is a third-born child with an older sister and older brother. Barbara liked to tease others and appeared a little bossy, very tough and intimidating. This, we know, is that outer shell to protect herself. Barbara is great at picking up vibes from people and can easily figure them out.

THIRD-BORN BOY WITH SECOND-BORN SISTER AND FIRST-BORN BROTHER

Here the third-born boy won't have to put up with as much sibling rivalry tension, as it is more difficult for the second-born girl to move up to the first position. She is special as the first-born girl, so she may be comfortable in this position. Since this third-born is the second boy, he may decide to excel at sports if his older brother is good at academics. If the older brother is an athlete, he may try a different sport or just go his own way and find something different, such as art or music.

Life Stories

Gene Kelly, the theatrical dancer, was born in 1912, the third of five children. He had an older brother, Tim, and older sister, Jay. Gene was one of

Hollywood's greatest dancers. Gene was giving dancing lessons at age sixteen, showing early his natural ability to dance and create. (The arts are a perfect outlet for the creative energies of a third-born.)

Walter Payton, nicknamed "Sweetness," was a running back for the Chicago Bears. Was his nickname because of his personality or his running style? His career rushing record of 16,726 yards is an all-time high in the National Football League and won him a place in the Hall of Fame. Born in 1954, he had an older brother, Eddie, who also played football and is now the head golf coach at Jackson State University, and an older sister, Pamela, who was the number-two child. While in high school Walter didn't want to compete with Eddie, who was the star running back, so he became a long jumper on the track team instead. It was only after Eddie graduated that Walter took up and excelled at football. Before that, his interest was in playing the drums and becoming a musician, showing the more artistic and creative side of his personality. After football, he showed his true caring side by supporting many charities with the Walter Payton Foundation. He would donate autographed memorabilia to churches, schools, and social service agencies to help them raise money.

Robert Blake had a brother who was three years older and a sister, Jovanni, who was the second-born. His parents decided to turn the children into an act called "The Three Little Hillbillys" when Robert was only three years old. The act was a failure, but Robert got into the acting profession after the family moved from New Jersey to Los Angeles. His big break was in the *Our Gang* films when he was six years old. He reports a miserable home life and says he was abused by an alcoholic father. He started school at the age of ten but then ran away

What's His Name?

He's the third-born child and had two older sisters, Anna and Corinne. His father was quite wealthy and gave to many humanitarian causes. His mother was from the South and had sympathy for the Southern cause. He was a sickly child who had asthma, so he spent a lot of time at home. He got interested in the outdoors and animals. He even got into taxonomy and carried this interest into his adult life. His father told him that he would have to work to get healthy, so he did. He became strong and quite an outdoorsman. He fought in several wars and led his own men into battle. He was the first U.S. president to fly in an airplane and submerge in a submarine. You know him as the twenty-fifth president, Theodore "Teddy" Roosevelt Jr.

from home at age fourteen. After serving in the Army he came back to Hollywood and turned his life around. He is most famous for his role as Tony Baretta. He was addicted to heroin, which he quit, and was later implicated in the death of his second wife, Bonnie Bakley, of which he was acquitted. He is definitely one of those threes with a hard outer shell for protection of his true emotional side.

THIRD-BORN BOY WITH SECOND-BORN BROTHER AND FIRST-BORN SISTER

This third-born has a brother directly above him, and has to grow up with a tough outer skin or other defenses because he is going to be picked on. The number two has issues with the older sister and is usually trying to move up the birth order ladder. If he moves up quickly and dethrones the older sister, things will be a lot easier for number three. The other possibility is that the brothers ignore their older sister and form a two-boy unit. The older boy can then become the academic and the younger boy the athlete, and then each gets his own identity.

My father was a third-born, with an older brother and the oldest a sister. He had a career as an educator and also worked as a naturalist, showing the sensitive side of a three. As an educator and elementary principal, he started one of the first "gifted" programs in the country. In college and later in life he pursued tennis. When on the tennis court he was a completely transformed person, with an overwhelming desire to win. He did win many state championships, the last coming when he was over forty years old. He was definitely more athletic than his older brother. When the school year was over, he had a choice to either work another month and take a four-week paid vacation or take an eight-week unpaid vacation. He always took the eight weeks. Reflecting on that time, I now see that the time spent in the woods on our summer vacations was more important to him than the money.

Life Stories

We all remember comedian Chris Farley. His sister, Barbara, is the oldest, and his older brother, Tom Jr., was the number-two child. As number three, Chris didn't have a chance to move up but put up a great defense by becoming a comedian. The phrase "laughing on the outside and crying on the inside" really was true for Chris, who was described as having a sweet vulnerability. He was the class clown and a natural athlete, despite his weight problem. He compensated for his shyness by being very loud, but was in inner turmoil and had an addictive personality. This is what led to his untimely death. Friends say he was very religious, which is not uncommon with third-borns.

THIRD-BORN GIRL WITH SECOND-BORN GIRL AND FIRST-BORN BOY

In this family, the two girls, numbers two and three, can hang together and be protected by big brother or just ignore him and do their own thing. By their own thing I mean they arrange themselves as a one and a two, letting big brother do his own thing. This would make the number-two girl the academic and number three the athlete. If number two competes with her older brother, then her younger sister can be her support. It can be the girls against the older brother, or the third girl can turn on her sister and go with the power by supporting her older brother.

Life Stories

Former tennis star Chris Evert has just this position. She has an older brother, Drew, and an older sister, Jeanne. She took the athletic path and really excelled. Although she showed the public a player with "ice" in her veins, she also showed a softer side as she made friends with most of her opponents.

Ruth Carter Stapleton was President Jimmy Carter's younger sister. She became an evangelist; the religious nature of the third child is a recurring theme. Ruth was so good at what she did that she even got Larry Flint, a first-born and the editor of *Hustler* magazine, to "find Jesus"—albeit it was only a one-year flirtation.

FINAL THOUGHTS ON THE THIRD-BORN #3

It's so important not to push children in directions they don't want to go, especially a third-born. Each child is different and if left to make decisions on his own will show you his way. The examples of third-borns in society really demonstrate what I mean by the variation of their choices of work.

The third child is the sensitive flower with the coat of armor. A sponge for the emotions around them, they are just the people to add the caring touch to our society. What is happening above them between the two older siblings, no matter what gender, can really affect their personality characteristics.

An understanding family is most important to the third-born, as they naturally absorb the feelings of those around them. If they are the first boy or girl, they have a greater burden to carry, as they must fulfill the family's expected role for the gender of that child. They develop a protective shell for their vulnerable emotional side. This hard shell can make the number three look very different from what he really is. In life, they will seek out ways to help people, maybe in the healing sciences, or get involved in creative fields of art or entertainment. Left alone, they develop a gentle approach to life. Some see them as dreamers, but many third-borns see their dreams come true.

Third-Borns

André the Giant	Chris Farley	Rosie O'Donnell
Tim Allen	James Garner	Jack Palance
Meredith Baxter	Tom Hanks	Sarah Palin
Robert Blake	Leona Helmsley	Walter Payton
Peter Boyle Jr.	Hulk Hogan	Norman H. Schwarzkopf
Marlon Brando Jr.	Gene Kelly	Charlie Sheen
Barbara Bush	Grace Kelly	Ruth Carter Stapleton
Macaulay Caulkin	Bob Kerry	Mother Teresa
Dwight Eisenhower	Madonna	
Chris Evert	Leslie Nielsen	

8

EVERYBODY KNOWS WHO I AM

The Three/Only

THE DRAMA KING OR QUEEN AND THE SOCIAL BUTTERFLY
THE THREE /ONLY #3/0

If there is one birth order that is difficult to understand, it's the three/only. This occurs when there are four or more years between the second child and the third child, and no other siblings for at least four years. The three/only birth order is difficult both for the person who carries it and for those who want to understand him.

Why is this so difficult? First there are, in most cases, fourteen different personal interactions that three/onlies must understand in their own family. Next, they carry two very dissimilar birth orders: the third child and only child. The only's influence *powers up* the characteristics of the third child, so to speak. Their emotions just well up within them and seem to boil over. This is a cocktail that definitely should be stirred, not shaken!

The three/only has the third-born's sensitivity, creative energy, and the need to work with groups of people. At the same time, he has the no-nonsense practical attitude of the only child, willing to go it alone and follow a more traditional course of action. If he can balance these two birth orders, we find a very interesting, creative person who seems to accomplish the impossible.

This child must identify with one of his parents as the person he can rely on for support and guidance. This is true of all the double birth orders that incorporate the only distinction. It's especially true for three/onlies because of their sensitivity to the world and others around them. As we will see, as adults they can combine their understanding of people and their power to control them.

Brothers and Sisters and the Gender of the Three/Only

If this child is the first of their gender in the family, they can be that long-sought boy or girl that mom or dad has been waiting for. Their dream has come true, but if the parents are not careful, the result can fall short of their expectations. If this third child has both an older brother and older sister, then he may be that "surprise" child no one expected. This situation involves other psychological considerations, but most important, the parents can give this child lots of attention just like an only child.

These two very different birth orders can create great conflicts for three/onlies. The switching back and forth between their two personalities is difficult for them and the people around them. When I see this birth order in children, I see a sensitive child who controls the situation through the use of emotion. Where the third-born is shy, the three/only demands that you understand his sensitivity. They are masters at changing the subject when they fall short of the mark. I call the girls my "drama queens," since they like to show

What's His Name?

He was born in 1889 and was the only child in the house until the age of five. He had two grown siblings from his father's first marriage. History reports that he was breast-fed for five years and that his mother was very protective, as she had lost a number of children before he was born. This three/only had an uncanny ability to understand and read the pulse of the people. He used this ability to manipulate his own countrymen and take control of the government, utilizing both his only characteristics and the intuitiveness of a three. He saw a plan for social change, though history saw it much differently. His name was Adolf Hitler.

off. When they come into the office everything must stop, as they want to be the center of attention.

These children have the outspoken nature of the only child but approach things with the sensitivity of the third-born. They can be overly dramatic: life with them can feel like an emotional roller coaster, leaving you exhausted in your attempt to understand them. Using the intuitive powers of the third-born, however, they are masters at understanding you!

An example of the three/only's dramatic behavior is one of my special patients, Alice. Alice had two older siblings and it was up to Grandpa to bring her to her visits. When she would burst through the door, everyone knew Alice was here. Her scenes in the office were always the same. After brushing her teeth, she had to show everyone how clean they were. Next we had to decide the color of the rubber bands that would go around her braces. After deciding on a color or combination of colors, she had to ask the other patients if they liked them. When leaving the office she would usually change her mind about her colors and have to come back to change them. You can imagine the anguish of the staff and her long-suffering grandfather. She controlled all of us and was always center stage. A recent local newspaper article shows her as playing the leading female role in her high school senior play. What's next? Hollywood?

One mother described her three/only child like this: "One minute she's my perfect little lady and at other times she's my cuddly little bear cub."

If they are the first-born of their gender in the family, three/onlies will feel extra special. This only strengthens their control of the family situation.

Life Stories

Walter Liberace, the popular Las Vegas pianist, was the surviving twin of a third birth to his mother. He was born in 1919, five years after the birth of his sister, Angelina, in 1914, and eight years after his first-born brother, George. He had another brother, Rudolph, eleven years younger, born in 1930. Liberace's mother was very interested in the theater, and her influence was not lost on Walter. Three/onlies—like only children—are very influenced by their parents. As with the other double birth orders, mom and dad can usually spend a lot of time with these children.

The arts are the chosen form of expression for many three/onlies. Trained as a classical pianist, Walter took his own course and created a unique image. Dramatic is certainly the word to describe Liberace.

Suzanne Mahoney Somers shows all the characteristics of the three/only personality. The attendant drama and emotion is accepted more readily in a woman than in a man. Born in 1946, with a sister seven years older and a brother six years older, Suzanne has played her life out in dramatic fashion. As teenagers, she and a friend would dress up and go to a ritzy hotel and pretend they were wealthy, although the family was of only modest means. Her mother saved for her to go to a private Catholic girls' school, where she pretended to be wealthy. Not making any friends, she began writing herself fictitious love letters to get attention, but the nuns found them and, because of their content, expelled her from school. After high school things did not get any easier for this drama queen. She married, divorced, and got pregnant all while in her teenage years. She had a hard time supporting herself and her baby son, as she just couldn't hold down a job. Nor could she control her spending—she bought clothes instead of paying the rent and passed bad checks.

During this time she was having an affair with a married producer, who did eventually marry her ten years later. Her first real role was playing the girl in the T-Bird in the movie *American Graffiti*. Her agent said she was happy only when she was performing. Her big role on TV was in *Three's Company* but she lost that job when her husband took over as her agent and demanded $100,000 an episode. She has since bounced back as an exercise guru with her own line of exercise equipment. True to the power and drama of the three/only, she never forgave her father for his alcoholism and his abuse of the family. In later years, after he gave up alcohol, she demanded he write an apology to the family for his actions. She did this on her own, without the support of her siblings. It's difficult for a three/only to forgive and forget, as they take things so personally.

Wilbur Wright, the co-inventor of the first successful airplane, was a three/only with two older brothers: Reuchlin, six years older, and Lorin, four years older. (Orville was born four years after Wilbur and was the first to pilot the Wright Flyer.) Wilbur's inventive genius is unquestioned. He also used his executive ability, an only trait, to control the commercial aspects of their airplane, in keeping with the "bigger picture" seen by the third-born.

Politician Tip O'Neill demonstrates what can happen when you harness both the executive ability of an only and the ability to work with groups as a third-born. He was a three/only, six years younger than his sister, Mary Rose, and seven years younger than his older brother, William. As the Speaker of the U.S. House of Representatives, he found a perfect stage for a three/only to act his part. Talk about drama in the House of Representatives! He was a power player in government, but as is true of his third-born side, he never lost touch with his constituents in Massachusetts.

THE ONLY/THREE

When there are more than seven years between the third child and the second child, the child becomes an only/three. He performs more like an only child and less like a third-born. This is a much easier combination to balance.

Life Stories

Mystery director Alfred Hitchcock was an only/three, born in 1899, seven years younger than his sister, Ellen Kathleen, born in 1892, and nine years younger than his older brother, William, born in 1890. He tells a story that

Alfred Hitchcock

when he was six years old and had misbehaved, his father sent him to the police station with a note. The officer on duty locked him in a jail cell for an hour, telling him, "That's what we do to little boys who don't behave." Hitchcock said from that day on, he was always afraid of the police, and that it was the reason he never learned to drive.

Who hasn't seen one of Hitchcock's films and noticed the drama and suspense that build throughout the picture? He has us in his control at least for the length of the picture. Who can forget *Psycho*, *The Birds*, and *Vertigo*? His films are a reminder of his great creative abilities, but also show a man with a conflicted personal life, or at least not an ordinary one. He was a very controlling person, and the actress Tippi Hedren of *The Birds* finally split with him over his controlling attitude. It has been said that one of his favorite actresses was Grace Kelly, who almost came out of retirement just for him. This isn't so hard to believe, as her birth order was a three.

The hyperactive personality of comedian Robin Williams, to some, does not indicate a person who is calm and balanced. Seeing his success using his creativity, sensitivity, and executive ability, it is hard to ignore that he is special. He was born in 1952 and lived most of his life as an only child. His

What's Her Name?

She was born in 1928, the first girl and the third of three children. Her two older brothers were twelve and eight years older: John and George Jr. She was seen in the movies as both a sensitive little child, her three side, but could speak her lines like an adult, her only side—both very captivating. Her very controlling mother was definitely a "stage mom." After the birth of her first two sons, she wanted a daughter. She was told that if her husband had his tonsils removed they would conceive a girl. He had the operation but the tonsils grew back, and she made him get them removed again. That's when they conceived their daughter. Known as "Little Miss One Take," she was child actress Shirley Temple Black.

father, an executive for Ford Motor Company, provided the family with a thirty-room mansion in Michigan. Robin filled his days with imaginary friends, his dog, Duke, and a turtle, Carl. When he was ten years old he found out that he had two half-siblings, one each from both of his parents' first marriages. Todd was thirteen years older than Robin, from his dad's first marriage; Lauren was four years older, from his mom's first marriage. Neither lived with him for any length of time, but they had an effect on his life. Being the third child in the family, and the second child for each of his parents, he was not treated like an overprotected only child. He was, instead, left alone a good deal of the time and thus really developed his imagination.

Robin was reported to have had poor social skills when he entered school, and he tended to be shy. He soon overcame these problems and went out for the wrestling team. By his junior year in high school he was on his way to becoming president of his class. The family then moved to California, and the rest is history.

This next only/three got his birth order after the death of his older sister, the third-born, who died two years before he was born. This moved him up into her third birth order position when he was really the fourth-born in the family. The first-born in the family was fifteen years his senior and his next sibling was twelve years older. This placed him twelve years behind his closest older sibling and made him an only/three. This child was the "pet" of the family.

He taught Sunday school as a young man and was very attached to his mother, living with her until her death in 1931. This man is none other than J. Edgar Hoover, who became director of the FBI in 1924.

He was a difficult man to understand, as was corroborated by his co-workers. "The organization created by Hoover does not consider independent thought a privilege of its members, only Hoover has that right," said Hoover. The cleaning staff was terrified about moving anything on his desk when they cleaned. He was one of the first people to have an "instant-on" television, as he hated to wait for it to warm up. The difficulty in "reading" this man is evident in a story told by one of his agents. A stickler for perfect margins, Hoover wrote in the margin of a letter sent to him by the agent, "Watch your borders." For the next month the FBI watched both the Canadian and Mexican borders!

FINAL THOUGHTS ON THE THREE/ONLY #3/0

The three/onlies and only/threes can be very interesting people. In "normal," real-life situations, these people make wonderful parents. They can get very involved with their children's activities and in community affairs. They care about others, are not afraid to speak up, and are dramatic.

When assessing someone with this birth order, check the sex of the older children in the family. Is this child the first in the family of their gender? Next, determine the interval between the older and younger siblings to see whether you are dealing with a three/only or an only/three.

Last, don't forget the parents, who after three children with large spacing between them will be a little older. This might influence the "only" side of this child's personality and reflect the generational effect of the parents. The child usually will be extremely close to one of his parents, which seems to be necessary for his balance. When you add power to the creative, sensitive three, amazing things can occur.

Three/Onlies and Only/Threes					
Wilbur Wright	4yr	3/0	Alfred Hitchcock	7yr	0/3
Adolf Hitler	5yr	3/0	Shirley Temple Black	8yr	0/3
Walter Liberace	5yr	3/0	Sid Caesar	10yr	0/3
Andy Garcia	5yr	3/0	Jamie Lynn Spears	10yr	0/3
Tip O'Neill	6yr	3/0	J. Edgar Hoover	13yr	0/3
Suzanne Somers	6yr	3/0	Merle Haggard	14yr	0/3
Patti Davis	6yr	3/0	Nathan Lane	20yr	0/3

9

I JUST WANT TO HAVE FUN

The Fourth-Born

I'M BIG ENOUGH TO GO WITH YOU—I'M NOT THE BABY

> **Fourth-Born Characteristics**
>
> - True baby of the family
> - Educated by older siblings
> - Wants to be taken care of
> - Can be forgetful
> - Interacts well with adults
> - Outspoken
> - Can be a comedian

The fourth-born is truly the baby in the family. If you think birth order has no effect, just look at a family photo album: how many pictures do you see of the fourth-born as compared to the older children? I rest my case.

You would think that this child is so far down the line from his three other siblings that he may be overlooked in the competition for parental attention. Not a chance—this child is usually the loudest of all the children. mom and dad are now really outnumbered, and their attention is divided among four children. This "baby" lets them know he's there!

The fourth child is almost raised by his older siblings. He gets a head start in school because he is taught by his older brothers and sisters. For this reason, some fourth-borns pursue higher education—going further than their older siblings. He gets along very well with older people; he has a lot of experience with his older siblings, and he is good at manipulation. Fourth-born children are the "baby" in the family and can become the comedians. Everyone looks out for the "baby," which can make the fourth child forgetful and unreliable when there is no one around to help him.

As with all the other birth orders, there is a flip side. Some fourth-borns can appear quite serious, especially if they perceive life as being very difficult and want to be successful. They know that they have to work hard when their older brothers or sisters are not there to help them.

In our office, these children are fun to treat. They seem to shift all their problems to someone else, and just breeze through life having fun. We rarely see their parents—an older sibling usually brings them to the office. These children can slip under the radar of their parents' watchful eyes and can also be outside the circle of sibling rivalry. As adults on their own, life appears to be hard work for them. This may be because early in life their paths were cleared by their older siblings.

I remember one fourth-born child who pulled me aside after we decided it was time for her braces. She said, "Isn't there a pill or something that I can take to make my teeth straight?" Unfortunately, there was no easy way for her. Adult patients can easily be identified as fourth-borns when they request flashy colors for their braces, just like their younger fourth-born counterparts.

I'll always remember a fourth-born patient who was a schoolteacher. After each appointment she couldn't wait to show her students her latest color combinations. A friend of mine is the fourth-born boy in his family. Now retired, he is having the time of his life riding motorcycles through Europe and enjoying his grandchildren. When it comes to his finances, he says, "I don't know much about them. I just leave them to someone else; as long as I get my check each month." About work, he says, "I tried it once and that was enough."

Gender and Position of the Fourth-Born

Just as with second- and third-borns, gender and family position are important to the development of the fourth-born. Being the only boy or girl in this large family really makes you special. You may be the long-desired boy or girl, and mom and dad can now stop growing the family. If this is you, you are certainly something special for your family. The attention you will receive from your siblings can be a great source of protection—or resentment, since you will be getting more of your parents' attention. When you are not the first of your gender, then all types of combinations are present, and with so many children anything is possible. Remember, all of this is true only if all the children are less than four years apart.

These are the possible gender combinations with fourth-borns:

Fourth-Born Gender Combinations: Oldest Boy

	4A	4B	4C	4D	4E	4F	4G	4H
#1	Boy	Boy	Boy	Boy	Boy	Boy	Boy	Boy
#2	Boy	Boy	Boy	Boy	Girl	Girl	Girl	Girl
#3	Boy	Girl	Girl	Boy	Boy	Girl	Boy	Girl
#4	Boy	Boy	Girl	Girl	Boy	Boy	Girl	Girl

Fourth-Born Gender Combinations: Oldest Girl

	4I	4J	4K	4L	4M	4N	4O	4P
#1	Girl	Girl	Girl	Girl	Girl	Girl	Girl	Girl
#2	Girl	Girl	Girl	Boy	Boy	Girl	Boy	Boy
#3	Girl	Girl	Boy	Girl	Girl	Boy	Boy	Boy
#4	Girl	Boy	Girl	Boy	Girl	Boy	Girl	Boy

As you can see, we have sixteen possible combinations! All kinds of alliances can develop with four children in the family. I suggest you look back to the section on the third-born to get a feel for how gender differences affect the siblings. The one unusual characteristic of the family of four is that the number-two child seems to have a better relationship with the number-four child than the others. This seems to work even if there are gender differences. It could be that number two doesn't want to be told what to do and number four doesn't mind being told what to do. The second-born can use a little of the "direction" he has been getting from number one and try it on number four.

Life Stories

Country singer and actress Dolly Parton, born in 1946 as the fourth of twelve children, has an older sister and two older brothers. Dolly has never taken herself very seriously and projects a certain childlike quality. I remember seeing her on the *Johnny Carson Show* with a book titled *Everything You Want to Know About Fashion*, by Dolly Parton. When Johnny opened it, he found the book full of blank pages. That's Dolly, not taking herself too seriously.

Actress Heather Locklear is the youngest of four children, born in 1961 in Canoga Park, California, a real "Valley Girl." She is really at her best in comedic roles, as seen in the TV show *Spin City*. She's been married twice, both times to rock stars: first to Tommy Lee of Motley Crüe, and then to Richie Sambora of Bon Jovi. Doesn't that say something about her staying young and having fun?

Actor Kirk Douglas was born Issur Danielovitch Demsky in 1916, the fourth of seven children and the first and only boy in the family. Kirk has played many macho roles, but underneath it all, he is truly the fourth child

What's Her Name?

When she was born she had three older brothers. They came from a very conservative family that believed in family values. Her dad was a political science university professor who ran for the state legislature and won. He then ran for Congress as a John Birch conservative from California and won that race too. His fourth-born daughter used to go to his office and he would show her off to all his friends. When he ran for Senate, it was disclosed that he had two children with one of his former students. His daughter became a wild child in high school and got pregnant in college. She got married and had to finish her teaching degree after she had the baby. Everybody said she was a great teacher and all the kids wanted to be in her class. She then had an affair with a thirteen-year-old student. He was also a fourth-born and had three older brothers. She was convicted of statutory rape and sent to prison for seven years. She is Mary Kay Letourneau. After prison and one more baby, she and Vili, her former student, got married.

who likes to have fun and let others take care of the details. One of his best friends in the business was Burt Lancaster, also a fourth-born child.

Writer and humorist Art Buchwald exhibited all the characteristics of a fourth-born. His mother was committed to a mental hospital four months after his birth, and he and his three older sisters were placed in foster homes. Although they were separated at times, they each demonstrated their birth orders. The oldest, Alice, was bossy, and the second child, Edith, was less assertive. The third, Doris, was very sensitive to everything around her and became a nurse. Art bluffed his way into the Army and World War II, getting a drunk to sign his induction papers. He started college in California having never graduated from high school. He became a newspaper man in Paris with very little experience but with a good "line." Of course, who can deny his humor and wit—a trait of the fourth-born? The humor of the fourth-born is never mean or dispirited; it's more of a little jab to wake you up. On the home front they act more like their children. Art's wife said he was not much of a disciplinarian—just a kid a heart. He even joked about his own death and dying in his last book *Too Soon to Say Goodbye*. He said, "Doctors gave me three weeks to live. I never knew dying could be so much fun." Having fun to the very end…only a fourth-born could see life this way.

We can't finish the fourth birth order without mentioning one of the greatest athletes and game players of our time, basketball player Michael Jordan. He was born in 1963, the fourth of five children. He has two older brothers and one older sister. He grew taller than anyone else in the family, and basketball was his game. After reaching the top of the basketball world, he retired and went on to play baseball. Then he returned to basketball and eventually owned and managed a team. This last endeavor was not a natural one for a fourth-born who loves to play games. He is now back to playing and coaching his basketball team, which is more suited to his natural ability.

FINAL THOUGHTS ON THE FOURTH-BORN

Fourth-borns are the game players of the birth order series. They like to have

Michael Jordan

fun, and if life is a game, that's even better. If someone is around to take care of them and let them play, better yet. They like to be around older people and can have the "gift of gab," bluffing their way though life. They are "people persons," and get along great with others, especially if they like having a good time. They can also be very hard workers who try to take life seriously. This is especially true if they see life as a challenge to overcome.

Fourth-borns will always try to see the fun in whatever they are doing. The life of the fourth-born is a little different if they are the first girl or boy. If he's a boy, there is a lot of pressure to be like a first-born, and that is a tough one for this birth order. If the fourth-born is the first girl, everybody takes care of her. She has three big brothers to protect her and clear the way. As an adult she will look for this same type of relationship.

The fourth-born can appear to be brash and very direct when asking questions, especially to older people. The manner and forthrightness of the questions may catch them off-guard. These people have a lot of experience talking to their much older siblings, so they appear to have little fear of authority figures.

Fourth-Borns		
Milton Berle	Mohandas Gandhi	Mary Kay Letourneau
Clint Black	Patricia Heaton	Ralph Nader
Art Buchwald	Michael Jordan	Dolly Parton
Kirk Douglas	Olga Korbut	Tim Robbins

10

IN CHARGE, BUT WITH FUN

The Four/Only

THE FOUR/ONLY #4/0

This can be considered the last of our traditional birth orders, the double birth order of the four/only. This is the child in the family who has three older brothers or sisters, with the third sibling at least four years or four school years older than himself. In some ways, people with this double birth order have the greatest potential for success—if they can control their two very disparate birth orders. They have great potential to achieve academically, for the other children, much older, can help them. These older siblings may overprotect them and not let them experience real failure in life.

When the power of the only side of this birth order kicks in, this child acts like an adult. With adults he has no fear, but he also has the childlike demands of the fourth-born baby in the family. The three/only lets you know how he feels; the four/only yells it. These people can appear to be demanding children, and as adults seem very direct and outspoken. This allows them to have the ability to bluff their way through life if they desire. They can appear more competent than they really are. It seems as if they have a guide on each shoulder, giving them different commands. The only says, "Take charge. You don't need any help. You can do it yourself." The four says, "Help me, please. I'm too little to do it myself. Won't you do it for me?" You can see how confusing it can get for the person who has two very dissimilar birth orders.

When we see these children in the office, we encounter a child and an adult in the same person. Many times this child's three older siblings are grown, and he may have a parent come with him. His actions in the office are unique to this birth order. He can be very demanding but irresponsible at the same time. They say they understand and may even mimic what you say, so you think you are communicating. They then appear to forget everything they heard.

When the age difference between siblings gets progressively greater than four years, the two birth orders (the four and only) get easier to handle. The four/only become more like an only and less like a four. It's difficult finding examples of this birth order in today's families. First, because of the trend toward smaller families, there are not as many fourth-born children. Second, there has to be a big gap between the third child and the birth of the fourth child. (This fourth child is sometimes referred to lovingly as the "surprise" because they come so late in life.)

Life Stories

Actress Jodie Foster has a four/only birth order. She was born in 1962, after her parents divorced, and five years after her brother, Buddy, was born in 1957. She has two older sisters: Lucinda, born in 1954, and Constance, born in 1955. Jodie's movie career has been an interesting one. She portrayed a childlike prostitute in *Taxi*. It was interesting for her birth order to play a character with both adult and child characteristics. She then played an investigator in the *Silence of the Lambs*. In real life she was the infatuation of John Hinkley Jr., the man who shot President Reagan. Her personal life has been a bit unconventional, as she decided to have a child on her own. It appears she is very much in control of her career demonstrating the only side of her double birth order.

Jodie Foster

Only/Fours

President Jimmy Carter's brother Billy, whom we might call an only/four, was eight years younger than his third sister, Ruth. His behavior was very embarrassing while his older brother was president. Do you remember Billy Beer? It's said that he never forgave his brother for not letting him manage the peanut farm while Jimmy was president. Jimmy just didn't think Billy was up to the task, and Billy never forgave him for his lack of confidence. Jimmy described Billy as a "people person," who was very unpretentious. He was always ready for a beer or a party!

Thomas Alva Edison, one of the world's greatest inventors, was an only/four. Born in 1847, he was the seventh birth in the family; the fourth, fifth, and

> ## What's His Name?
>
> **He was born in West Virginia** when his mother was forty years old. At that time he had three grown brothers, the youngest of whom acted as a surrogate father. He was very sickly as a child and as an adult felt that he was always a little ill. He had a lot of emotional anxiety left over from his childhood, as his father was mentally ill and died when he was thirteen. He became known as the class clown in school and really came out of his shell. He had several wives—each one younger than the last. His second wife said of him, "You just want to hold him in your arms and protect him." He was also known for his nervous laughter. He played the deputy sheriff on *The Andy Griffith Show* and in *The Shakiest Gun in the West*. You know him as the actor Jesse Donald Knotts.

sixth children died in childhood. This made Thomas fourteen years younger than the third child, Harriet Ann. Thomas was home-schooled and raised more as an only child. The great fourteen-year distance between his next oldest sibling left him at home with his mother. He had the great confidence of an only child, ready to go where no one else had ventured. At the same time, he had the curiosity of a child, typical of the number-four position. What a perfect combination for an inventor: playtime for the fourth-born and the temperament of the serious only child to control his inventions and build a business.

FINAL THOUGHTS ON THE FOUR/ONLY #4/0

Look carefully at those you think fit the four/only double birth order. With these larger families, a lot of different living arrangements can take place. Sometimes this child is raised by his older siblings. If the sex of this child is unique in the family, additional pressures will come to bear on him. If the fourth child is a boy and he is the only boy in the family he may be asked to fill the role of the first born which would be difficult for this birth order.

If there are others of the same sex in the family, then this child can really enjoy being the baby. He can get all the attention that an only child would receive. Masters at interpersonal relationships, four/onlies are the true "people persons." People with this birth order are very direct in their approach. As the "baby" in the family, they usually got what they wanted and had many surrogate parents to demand from. If they are more of an only/four, life is easier to balance and they can easily achieve great things.

Four/Onlies and Only/Fours					
Ronald Reagan Jr.	6yr	4/0	Herb Kelleher	9yr	0/4
Jodie Foster	7yr	0/4	Thomas Alva Edison	14yr	0/4
Billy Carter	8yr	0/4	Jessie Donald Knotts	17yr	0/4
Burt Lancaster	9yr	0/4			

11

THE FAMILY WITHIN A FAMILY

More Double Birth Orders

WHAT HAPPENS WHEN YOU SPACE
THE BIRTH OF YOUR CHILDREN

Just when you thought we were through describing all the birth orders, here come a few more. We have covered the only child, first-born, one/only, second-born, two/only, third-born, three/only, fourth-born, and four/only. For some of you, we have yet to describe your birth order. I have not forgotten you. We first had to cover the basics before we got to the "family within the family"

If there is a four-year or greater space between siblings, the double birth orders of one/only, two/only, three/only and four/only occur. (See Multiple Double Birth Orders on following page.) What happens if after the birth of the first child, four or more years pass, and then there are three more children? If these children are spaced closer than four years apart, you get the "family within a family."

In these situations, which can be called double ordinal birth orders, the first child is a one/only. The second child is the second birth but is also the oldest in the second family. He would then have the double birth order of

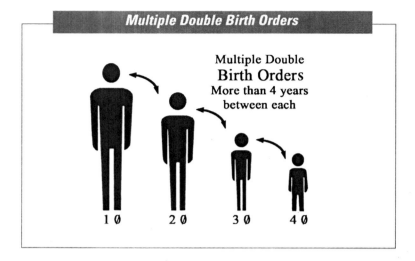

a 2/1. The next child is the third birth, but in this "second" family has the birth order of 3/2. The fourth birth is the third child in this "second family" and has a 4/3 birth order. (See Family Within a Family, below.) I treated a family of four girls with just this type of birth order spacing. First there was Pam, age twelve; Louise, age six; Ruth, age four; and Becky, age two. This made Pam a one/only, Louise a two/one, Ruth a three/two, and Becky a four/three.

If you come from a family with this type of spacing, you will easily understand this type of double birth order. My experience with these double birth orders reveals a child with fewer internal conflicts than the double birth orders combined with "only" characteristics. Internal conflicts may also be decreased because these children have fewer differences

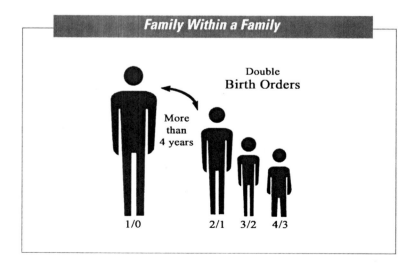

Four Girls with Double Birth Orders

between their two birth orders. This is true when the double ordinal birth orders are just one number apart, i.e., 2/1, 3/2, 4/3.

As we have seen, most children want to move up in birth order, if given the opportunity. These "family within a family" children get a chance to move up without displacing anyone. They each carry a higher and lower birth order. The characteristics of people with this type of "family within a family" double birth order seem to show an even blending of each component birth order. The birth order traits appear in a random manner, without any becoming dominant. When these double ordinal birth orders are greater than one number apart—i.e., 3/1, 4/1—they can create some very fascinating people.

Life Stories

Walt Disney was a four/one. The four gave him the childlike vision and the one gave him the executive power to pull it all off. Walt had three older brothers—Herbert, born in 1888; Raymond, in 1889; and Roy, in 1893. Walt was born in 1901, eight years after Roy. His sister, Flora, arrived in 1903. This made Walt the oldest in the second family.

Balancing these two very different birth orders was difficult for Walt, who battled depression all his life. Those closest to him found him difficult to understand, as he vacillated between his fourth-born and first-born personalities. He has been accused of trying to take all the credit for the Disney creations and characters. He rarely gave credit to his artists and creative story writers, which did not help morale at the Disney studios. He was also a very vindictive person who made others pay the price for going against his wishes. This first-born side made him very patriarchal and controlling

Walt Disney

toward his employees, who saw him as stern and conservative. He could never understand why they wanted a union to represent them.

Walt's fourth-born side was more playful and childlike. He even had his own miniature railroad that he would ride around his house and property. Sometimes this playful side ran into his more conservative nature with embarrassing consequences. At the premiere of *Pinocchio*, he hired eleven little people dressed in Pinocchio outfits to stand on the roof of the theater above the marquee. Someone sent up a few quarts of liquor, and by three o'clock in the afternoon the crowd in the street saw eleven naked little people playing craps on top of the marquee, much to Walt's embarrassment.

Business tycoon Donald Trump shares the four/one birth order. He has two older sisters and one older brother, born ten years before him. Following Donald came a brother, Robert, two years later. This puts the two boys in their own "family within a family." Donald is known as the P. T. Barnum of real estate and is a true self-promoter. (Talk about bluffing!) He says, "The real excitement is playing the game." Just as Walt Disney had amusement parks, Donald has casinos and beauty pageants. That's the four side of his birth order. A gifted athlete, he came close to playing professional baseball. As a child he was known to his brothers and sisters as "The Great I AM," and never respected authority. Again, the adult is not much different than the child.

Princess Diana had a three/one double birth order. She had two older sisters, Sarah and Jane, four and six years older than she. This made her a three, and with the birth of her younger brother, she added the one birth order. What an interesting combination! She wanted to be in charge and give orders like a number one, which put her in conflict with the royals. The three side of her personality—her sensitivity—was expressed by her interested in the disadvantaged. She was a champion against the use of landmines and to those who had been harmed by them. She also revealed her vulnerability when confronted with her personal crises. Was she the image of a damsel in distress? Remembering the final words of her younger brother (a four/two birth order) at her funeral gives you an insight into another double birth order. He was hostile toward the royal family. As a number four, he was not afraid to speak his mind on behalf of his sister. As the only son in the family, he may perceive his position as that of family protector.

Princess Diana

Guess who also shares this birth order? The little pixie formerly of the *Today Show* and now anchor of *CBS Evening News*, Katie Couric. Katie has two older sisters, five and eight years older, making her a third-born. Then comes a brother two years younger, making her the first-born in this second family. It's interesting to note that she has the same gender distribution of siblings as that of Princess Diana.

FINAL THOUGHTS ON DOUBLE ORDINAL BIRTH ORDERS

The combinations of the ordinal birth orders can create some interesting people. The differences don't appear to be as dramatic as combinations with an only birth order, but are complicated nevertheless. You can now see how the individual birth orders express themselves in combinations. People with double ordinal birth orders are quite unique, made so by their blended personality characteristics.

Double Ordinal Birth Orders (Family Within a Family)			
Will Smith	2/1	Walt Disney	4/1
Owen Wilson	2/1	Donald Trump	4/1
George Hamilton	2/1	Orville Wright	4/1
George Washington	3/1	Carolyn Bessette Kennedy	3/2
Harry Houdini	3/1		
Katie Couric	3/1		
Princess Diana	3/1	Pauline Esther Friedman	
Esther Pauline Friedman		(Abigail Van Buren)	3/2
(Ann Landers)	3/1	Teri Garr	3/2
Wyatt Earp	3/1		

12

BIRTH ORDERS BEYOND NUMBER FOUR

FOR THE **REALLY** BIG FAMILIES

Some of you must be very perplexed by now if you come from really big families. Why, you ask, have I waited this long to talk about those of you who are #5, #6, #7, #8, #9, and beyond? Simply because in today's society there are not many of you.

Years ago large families were the norm when most people lived on farms and children were needed to plant and harvest the crops. In China large families were a source of social security, because at least one of the children would probably be successful and support the parents in their old age. In 1979 the Chinese government implemented the one-child policy. They have been giving incentives to those who will limit their families, such as free contraception, abortions, and sterilization; lower taxes; better schooling; and better housing. It seems to have worked, for the birth rate has declined from 5.7 to 1.9 births per couple. Still, a male child is favored as he has a better chance to earn a living and support the parents in their old age. Now, with only one child per family, an adult married couple may have to support four elderly parents and their one child. The Chinese social security system is being forced to make changes to address this problem. Imagine a country with a billion only children, many of whom had parents who were also only children.

SECOND-LEVEL BIRTH ORDERS

Understanding the birth orders beyond #4 is much simpler than it may seem. After the first set of four birth orders (1, 2, 3, and 4), the second set is 5, 6, 7, and 8. This is assuming there are fewer than four years between each successive sibling, with no gaps of four years or greater even in the first group of 1, 2, 3, and 4. If there are large gaps of four years or more, you get the "family within the family" that we discussed in the preceding chapter.

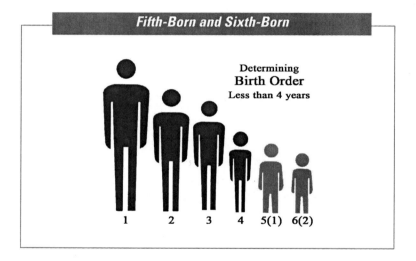

Fifth-Born and Sixth-Born

Determining
Birth Order
Less than 4 years

1   2   3   4   5(1)   6(2)

Fifth-Born and Sixth-Born

Fifth-Born #5
- If born within four years of fourth-born sibling, birth order will start over again;
- therefore, fifth born is similar to a first-born
- 5(1)

Sixth-Born #6
- If born within four years of fifth-born
- Birth order has started over again with fifth-born as a 5(1)
- Sixth-born is then similar to a second-born
- 6(2)

What's His Name?

He was born the eighth of nine children. His family lived on a farm, but his older brothers said he never did any work, just loved to play. In school he told everybody he was going to be governor some day. He had a photographic memory and dropped out of high school to become a traveling salesman. He was a natural—everyone loved him and he could sell anything. He studied law and in less than a year passed the oral law board.

He became governor at age thirty-four and was a comedian, showman, and very outspoken. One of his girlfriends was a stripper. (The public didn't like that too much.) He was having so much fun that a number of people had him committed to a mental hospital, but as governor, he signed his own release. He was a U.S. senator and was planning his bid for the presidency of the United States when he was shot and killed at forty-two years old. He was Louisiana governor, Huey Pierce Long—also known as "The Kingfish."

This second group of four children share personality characteristics with their counterparts in the first group of four. Number 5 is similar to 1, number 6 is similar to 2, number 7 is similar to 3, and number 8 is similar to 4. Notice I said similar—not the same.

You might make the comparison between primary colors and secondary colors. These colors share the same hue, but not the intensity. It's the same for the second-level birth order positions. They are just not as intense as the first group. For example, if number one is very bossy, this trait is toned down in number five.

Jackie Roosevelt Robinson, the baseball player, was the fifth-born, with three older brothers and one older sister. Jackie was instrumental in the integration of Major League Baseball. He had the strength of a number one and also the ability to keep his anger under control. His drive to succeed was similar to a number one, just not as obvious.

Evolutionist Charles Darwin was the fifth in a line of six children. He waited many years to write his theory of evolution, as he did not want to anger those who controlled the trends in scientific thought in his day. He eventually published his work after getting support from fellow scientists before publication.

Number fives are not as pushy as number ones, but they still get the job done.

If you come from a really big family with siblings in the ninth, tenth, eleventh, or twelfth birth positions, the intensity of personality characteristics is even less than that of the second-level birth orders. When talking with people who come from larger families, it's always interesting to note who in the family they get along with the best. It should be no surprise that it is their counterpart birth order. A number nine relates best to numbers one and five. Number eleven seems to relate best to numbers three and seven.

Birth Orders Beyond Number Four			
Gracie Allen	#5	Michael Jackson	#7
Daniel Boone	#6	Florence Griffith Joyner	#7
Charles Bronson	#11	Bill Murray	#5
Glenn Cambell	#8	Soledad O'Brien	#5
Charles Darwin	#5	Jackie Robinson	#5
Dizzy Gillespie	#9	Sammy Sosa	#5
Alan Jackson	#5	Gertrude Stein	#5
Huey Pierce Long	#8	John Travolta	#6
Earl Long	#9		

13

MARRIAGE PARTNERS
AND BIRTH ORDER

IF YOU CAN KISS ENOUGH FROGS…A PRINCE?

A book on birth order cannot overlook the topic of marriage. What is the "magic" formula for a successful marriage? If I knew, I would give up my orthodontic practice and do premarital counseling. If birth order has such an influence on personality, then there must be a birth order connection to successful marriages, right? There is! Everyone wants a marriage that will last, so it doesn't surprise me when many future brides and grooms question me after each of my lectures. With 51 percent of all marriages ending in divorce, these people know the odds are against them and want to get an affirmation that theirs will be a long and happy marriage. There are also those who are divorced or are going through a divorce, and they

Maybe a prince?

want advice too. I remember one man who couldn't wait until I finished my lecture and came up to me at a break. He said, "If only I had heard your talk before I got married. You described my wife—did you know her?" I knew I was safe with my answer of "no." "Well," he said, "I'm a one and she was a two/only. I could never make her happy until the day of our divorce, and she got half the estate and our house. If only I had heard you sooner."

Find Your Brother or Sister

I'm not suggesting incest. What I am saying is find a man or woman who mirrors your family sibling situation when you were growing up. If you had brothers or sisters, you unconsciously became familiar with the characteristics that coincide with their birth orders. This makes you more knowledgeable, in an intuitive sense, about others who share your siblings' birth orders. If you mimic your childhood birth order pattern, you are almost guaranteed a long marriage. What do I mean by mimic? If there are two children in the family, the older a boy and two years later a girl, then the boy is a number one and the girl a number two. The boy should marry a number-two girl who has a number-one older brother. His sister should marry a number-one boy who has a number-two younger sister. Why does this seem to work? You spend many years with your siblings, learning to live with their different birth order characteristics. As an adult, if you come across someone with one of your siblings' birth orders, you have a very good chance of understanding that person. You already know the "fingerprint" of their personality. You don't need to have had a good relationship with your sibling for a romantic relationship to work. Just the fact that you know the specific birth order is enough. These types of marriages are very, very easy on both parties. Each partner just seems to know the other so well. It might even be one type of "love at first sight."

> If both you and your mate mimic each other's sibling
> birth order = SUCCESS!

What happens when one partner mimics his childhood birth order but the other does not? He or she has the easier time in the marriage; the other spouse has more trouble adjusting and "reading" the mate.

How does this work if you are from a family with all boys or girls? You have some understanding of the different birth orders, but gender does color personality. It's a match, but it's not perfect.

Parents and the Selection of a Partner

We have all heard the saying that a boy picks a girl like his mother and a girl picks a husband like her father. Again, we have to look at birth order for this "recognition" of your future mate. Although parents are the dominant force in the life of an only child, their influence can also be strong in people who have double birth orders. Parents will have a greater influence on the rearing of these children. The child will pick up on the birth orders of the parents and may gravitate to a mate with a similar birth order. If you come from a family with a number of closely spaced siblings, you will still have an additional understanding of your parents' birth orders. This could be the little kernel of recognition you see in a potential partner.

Love at First Sight

Does this mean that the phrase "love at first sight" describes what happens when you find someone who mimics the birth order of a brother or sister in your family? It may be one type of love at first sight. There is another type, however, that can be more powerful than just seeing one of your siblings' birth orders. It's the feeling you get when you see another *you*—when you find someone who shares your birth order. It's kind of like looking into a mirror—you *really* know this person. The problem is that there can be only one image reflected in the mirror. Who will be out front? As time goes by, one person has to give in to the other or friction will end the union. You might now be thinking that your marriage doesn't fit this mimicking thing. Why are you and your spouse successful? My answer is that any and all combinations can beat the odds—it's just that some combinations are much easier and take less work. You might want to think about who plays the dominant role in the marriage. (This also applies to any partnership.) In the simplest terms, the power order of the traditional birth orders is: only, first-born, second-born, third-born, fourth-born.

It gets much more complicated when you combine people with double birth orders together, or single birth order people with double birth order people. Each of these people has embedded in their personality the most powerful birth order: the only! The interval between siblings will determine just how much the only personality will express itself. At four years apart, each personality of the double birth order is expressed about 50 percent. As the years increase between siblings, the only characteristics become more dominant. You might say if you marry someone with a double birth order you really marry two people. What a deal!

A friend of mine said that it is very easy to test who has the power in the marriage: when the couple is just getting into bed, one of them notices a light on in the kitchen, or that the cat is still outside, or any number of things that were not done. The person who gets up to do the chore has the less dominant birth order or has given in to the other. Mr. or Ms. Dominant remains in bed.

One of my editors said, "I disagree. I'm a one and my husband is a four, and I'm always the one to get up. I'm just more anal about household stuff than he is. I think you could view this the opposite way: the one who gets up is the dominant one who's in charge of the house. The subordinate lazes around in bed knowing that someone else is in charge and will do the necessary work."

To answer her I guess I should have said this little test would be best used by a married couple who have the *same* birth order. In her case she is a one and her husband is a four. Everyone does things for a number four and have all their life. I couldn't have picked a better example. Always remember the lower birth orders have a lot of practice at manipulating the birth orders above themselves.

Love Blooms in the Orthodontic Office

I have witnessed some very interesting situations when dealing with patients at the peak of their teenage hormonal surges. Passing notes back and forth in their toothbrush cases can be the start of a budding romance. The patient with the higher birth order often controls the situation. Jimmy and Sara were treated at the same time and then went off to college together. I remember hearing about the on and off of their relationship when I would see them yearly to check their retainers. I always knew the romance was on when they came in together. After graduation they sent me their wedding picture. Their birth orders? He was a fourth-born, with a number-two older sister. She is a number two with a older brother. It has been much easier for him, as he has mimicked his childhood birth order, but she has been having problems in the marriage trying to control this "fun" number four.

Life Stories

Former president George Herbert Walker Bush and his wife, Barbara Pierce Bush, are a perfect mimicking match. This marriage has lasted over fifty years, solving more than the average number of life's problems. George, a number two, has an older brother and a younger sister. Barbara is a number three with two older siblings, a number-one sister and a number-two brother. They met at a college dance, and at least one of them knew instantly that it was *love at first sight!*

Sibling Rivalry? At the Wedding?

You would think that sibling rivalry is all over with by the time your children are ready to wed, but think again. I get invited to a lot of weddings—I guess that's another benefit of being an orthodontist! Several years ago I was invited to the double wedding of two former patients, sisters Carol the first-born and Cynthia the second. They are only two years apart in age, but are in no way alike. This showed up in dramatic fashion at the wedding.

Carol was becoming a teacher like her husband. Cynthia picked a different direction, becoming an organic farmer with her husband, living without electricity in a back-to-nature environment. Their differences really showed up at the wedding. Carol had the traditional service, with bridesmaids and escorts in the full wedding attire. Cynthia had a few bridesmaids in "natural" attire, with flowers in their hair, and a guitar player. No shoes were evident in Cynthia's bridal party. The food was another matter. One side of the table had all-natural food and a vegetarian menu, while the other side had more traditional wedding fare. Sibling rivalry never ends—children always want to be different and have their own identity. The latest I have heard is that Cynthia is two grandchildren ahead of her older sister.

DOES AGE REALLY MATTER?

The power in a relationship appears to have little to do with age superiority. This may explain the May-December marriages that are successful. Typically, the man is many years older, but today we see many couples in which the woman is the older partner. To understand the power balance in these relationships, one has to look at the only child in a family. In a family with only one child, where neither of the parents was an only child, this child can hold power over the parents. Birth order, not age, tips the balance of power.

May-December Unions

This familiar term describes two people who are many years apart in age and seem to have a normal marriage. Many critics would ask what can he see in such a young woman, or what does she see in that old man. Some would suggest that only money keeps them together. The same can be said for the older woman and younger man. History has shown that these relationships can really work, and they have been portrayed by the film industry for years.

Julie Andrews as Eliza Doolittle

The King and I (1956) puts the young teacher with the older king. *Sabrina* (1954) with Audrey Hepburn, Humphrey Bogart, and William Holden, pits brother against brother to win the hand of a woman thirty years younger. *My Fair Lady* (1964) depicts a twenty-five-year age difference between Eliza Doolittle and Henry Higgins. Of course, the woman can also be older, as was shown in the fifty-six-year difference in *Harold and Maude* (1971), with Ruth Gordon and Bud Cort. But what goes on in real life? Let's see if birth order is a factor.

Real May-December Unions

Once again we have to look at show business, as these are the people everyone loves to write about. Actress Susan Sarandon is fourteen years older than her actor companion, Tim Robbins. They met and fell in love on the movie set of *Bull Durham*. Susan is a number-one child, the oldest of eight siblings. Tim is a fourth-born and has an older sister. They each match or mimic their childhood birth orders. Tim's oldest sister was the first-born, and Susan had many younger brothers.

Actor Michael Douglas and actress Catherine Zeta-Jones are another May-December couple; they have a twenty-five-year age difference. Michael is the first-born, with a younger brother, Joel, born two years later. Catherine is a second-born, with an older brother, David, two years her senior. This marriage will be a lot easier on Catherine than on Michael, since she mimics her childhood sibling relationship. Although Michael has a younger sibling, the gender is reversed.

Actor Harrison Ford and actress Calista Flockhart are twenty-three years apart. Harrison is a first-born, with a younger brother, Terry, and Calista is a second-born, with an older brother, Gary. This relationship should be easier for her than for Harrison.

These first examples were couples who closely mimicked their childhood birth orders, but there are couples who appear to have the same birth orders. We call this couple *love at first sight*. In these situations, one of the partners has to take a back seat.

Actress Goldie Hawn and actor Kurt Russell are six years apart—Goldie is older. Both are second-borns and both have older sisters. These two very independent second-borns say that they never plan to officially marry. They both have children from earlier marriages and have one child together.

Silent screen star Charlie Chaplin was thirty-six years older than his wife, Oona O'Neill. Charlie was a two/only, with an older stepbrother, Sydney, four years his senior. Oona had a brother, Shane, six years her senior, making her a two/only as well. She was very devoted to Charlie and together they had eight children. She cared for him until he died in 1977 at age eighty-eight. She never remarried and died at age sixty-five in l991.

MARRIAGE PARTNERS FOR THE BIRTH ORDERS

Okay, you say, tell me a little bit more about each of the ordinal birth orders and how they might react in a marriage situation with the other birth orders. Do they have any unique characteristics that show up?

Onlies

The only child can come in many flavors, so look at his parents and see what their birth orders were. This person will be attracted to someone who shares a birth order with the parent he identifies with more. Many only children feel that they were the reason their parents had only one child, and want to make it up to their parents with a big family of their own. These people have usually gotten everything they wanted and don't know how to share, so beware. They may see you as one of their possessions and not let you have your independence.

The other side of an only is a bookish, introverted person who likes being alone. They may be very caught up in themselves and you could be along for the ride. An only can make a match with any birth order; it depends on their parents.

Here are a few onlies who are familiar to all of us. Can you see their "only" characteristics? Jack Lemmon, Frank Sinatra, Brooke Shields, Lisa Marie Presley, Jesse Jackson, Jerry Lewis, Condoleezza Rice, Charles Lindbergh, Howard Hughes Jr., Regis Philbin, and Tim Conway.

Ones

Ones are the power brokers in the birth order series. A lot of their personality will depend on how they handled the sibling rivalry, and who won. It also depends on what gender was the number two in the family. They generally want to tell people what to do, and this means *you*! They have carried this trait from their childhood. They also carried a few more things, especially the need to be perfect and do everything right. Always trying to measure up to someone else's standards is a tough burden to carry. They just love to be told they have done a good job. They also want to be the boss, so try not to get in their way.

The other side of the one is the person who will wait on you hand and foot to make you feel guilty that you are not grateful. This is just another way a number one will try to control the situation. They may not come off as bossy, but you will feel the effect of their power. If they marry a number two, the one should be careful not to tell the two what to do. If they marry a number three, let's hope they don't control him or her so much that the three can't be creative and express themselves. If they marry a number four, they just might find a person who will listen to what they have to say—even though the four may ignore them and blow it off and have fun.

Here are a few number ones with a mixture of younger siblings: Rush Limbaugh has a brother; Harrison Ford has a brother; Hillary Clinton has two younger brothers; Tommy Smothers has a brother; Johnnie Cochran has a sister;

Smothers Brothers

Jimmy Stewart had a sister; Sophia Loren has a sister; Humphrey Bogart had a sister; Sam Walton had a brother; George S. Patton had a sister; Henry Kissinger has a brother; Anthony Quinn had a sister; Raquel Welch has a brother; and Colonel Harland Sanders had a brother.

Twos

The wild card with the two is whether they dethroned number one and moved up to assume the throne. These people don't like to be told what to do. On the other hand, they won't be telling you what to do either. Just don't get in their space and always give them their freedom. Their interest in projects keeps them busy, although it may drive you crazy. Be mindful of the gender of the number-one sibling in their family.

These people will usually be athletes and will enjoy physical endeavors. Dirt and sweat are not foreign to them. Money is an attraction to these people for the independence that it brings, not for what it buys. They usually have great personalities—just don't try to move them in a direction they don't want to go. They can match up with a number one if they have dethroned their sibling. A third-born can be a good match, especially if they like the outdoors. A fourth-born is a very good match as he won't try to tell a number two what to do and he likes that.

A few examples of twos and their siblings are: Bob Dole has an older sister; John Kennedy Jr. had an older sister; Abraham Lincoln had an older sister; Donald Rumsfeld has an older sister; Martin Luther King Jr. had an older sister; Bill Gates has an older sister; Ronald Reagan had an older brother; Martha Stewart has an older brother; Jerry Seinfeld has an older sister; Warren Buffett has an older sister; Kathie Lee Gifford has an older brother; and Paul Newman had an older brother.

Threes

These very sensitive people have a protective shell, and they can show both a sweet, loving side and an emotionally distant one. Sibling rivalry doesn't have much of an effect on these people, but the genders above them do. If the number three is a boy and the only boy in the family, he will feel lots of pressure. If the third is a girl, she may be very overprotected by her older brothers and look for a similar relationship in marriage. Money is not important to these people; they have more of a global outlook and a sensitivity to those around them. For all the ladies, if you want a dance partner, then this is the birth order to look for. Threes love to dance and are good at it. These people must exercise their creative instincts and talents. A gentle approach is all-important to them. Enjoying nature and playing and working with groups are all traits of their birth order.

A match with a number one may work well as long as the three is not pushed too hard. The three may feed on the energy of a number two and get involved with creative projects. If matched with a number four, the relationship could become directionless, as the three is just not strong enough to get number four into gear.

Here are a few number threes and the genders of their older siblings: General Norman Schwarzkopf has two older sisters; Rosie O'Donnell has two older brothers; Chris Evert has an older brother and sister; Leslie Nielsen has two older brothers; Marlon Brando Jr. had two older sisters; Bob Kerrey, the politician, has two older brothers; President Dwight Eisenhower had two older brothers; Tom Hanks has an older brother and sister; and Chris Farley had an older sister and brother.

Fours

The true baby of the birth orders, fours have had the way cleared for them by older siblings, so they will look for a mate who will lead the way. Again, we must discover the gender of the older siblings. As the fourth child, if they are the first of their gender, they can be treated in a very special manner. Responsibility is not their thing but they will rise to the occasion if necessary. If they see life as very difficult, then worry will play a big part in the marriage if the other partner doesn't step up to the plate and lead. Playing and having fun in life is really the fourth-born's greatest asset. He can bluff his way through things, as he is very good with older people and large groups. These people tend to choose mates who are older than their peer group, possibly even choosing someone a generation older than themselves. If they choose a number one, they have picked the birth order that acts like a parent figure and who likes to tell others what to do. Twos match very well with fours because the four does not tell the two what to do and gives him space. A three and a four combination could be trouble if no one takes the lead and gives direction in the relationship.

A few examples of fourth-borns and their siblings are: Dolly Parton has one older sister and two older brothers; Michael Jordan has two older brothers and one older sister; Singer Clint Black has three older brothers; and Kirk Douglas has three older sisters.

COMBINATIONS OF SIMILAR BIRTH ORDERS

Okay, you ask, why didn't you tell us about married people with the same birth order? I was saving it for a special section. The dynamics can be so different that I didn't want to add to the confusion.

If you are married to someone with your same birth order, someone will have to give up their power to the other to make this marriage a success. Like birth orders attract at first, then have a power struggle.

When both mates are onlies or both are number ones, these couples make the ultimate power couples. The bossing around can become intense, so a division of duties is in order so each has something to control. They are in charge and organized.

Two twos might be busy making money and/or playing sports. Here again, someone must give in to the other. A couple can't always agree, and as the two doesn't like to be told what to do, one party must back down. Ideally they can compartmentalize their marriage with each taking responsibility for different aspects of their lives.

Two threes would have a wonderful time together saving the world—or dreaming about it. Someone must take charge and pay the bills and balance the checkbook. Two dreamers can have trouble remembering to pay the rent.

Two fours would be playing and having so much fun they might lose sight of reality. This could possibly be the couple who has to ask older siblings for the rent money. There is the possibility that if one of the fours in the couple sees things coming apart, he or she may rise to the occasion and take some responsibility.

14

FAMILY PLANNING

Spacing Your Children

DO YOU WANT ONE FAMILY? OR MANY LITTLE ONES?

Chapter Thirteen covered marriage. As the saying goes, *first comes love, then comes marriage, then comes the baby in the baby carriage.* What is the ideal spacing of your children? You may be in the parental planning stage and have the opportunity to determine the spacing of your children. Today, with modern methods of birth control and in vitro fertilization, conception can be planned for any desired sibling spacing.

A One and a Two and a Three

What is the ideal spacing? Determine whether you want a close, interactive family or a number of individual families of one child each so you can give them more nurturing. The most common reason for a four- or more year interval is that with greater spacing the family can recover financially between children and as a result have more monetary resources for each child. It's especially true for expensive higher education, when only one child would be in college at any time. There may be less sibling rivalry, as there is not as much interaction between the children when they are separated by four or more years. A four-year difference in age is magnified in childhood. For example, an eight-year-old would have little in common with a twelve- or thirteen-year-old sibling. Third, the early years of intense twenty-four-hour care is easier on the parents with one child at a time. Parents who are advocates of larger spacing also feel they can give more quality time to each child. Some parents don't plan at all until the first child is born and then opt for greater spacing because they need a rest after finding out how much work a new baby can be.

Proponents of closer spacing have their own list of reasons. When children are spaced fewer than four years apart (or are fewer than four school years apart) there is more true sibling interaction. The older children may even teach the younger ones. Both the good times and bad are recorded forever in everyone's mind and in the family photo album. It's easy to see that the first-born has the most pictures and the fourth-born the least!

Why does the closely spaced family seem to function as more of a unit? It's because of the close ages of the children. Each child tries to be different to secure his place in the family, and each has his unique role to play. Later in life, each child keeps his position in the family and as an adult can remember childhood interactions with older and younger brothers and sisters. With close spacing, toilet training, soccer, ballet, school events, and dental visits all seem to rush together in a dizzying spin and then they are off to college....Relief? Or did it go by so quickly that we really didn't get a chance to enjoy the whole process? That, of course, is what the proponents of larger sibling spacing would say.

Knowing about birth order may make you want to take a second look at the spacing you desire in your family. Gaps larger than four years with multiple children following the four year space will result in individual families within the larger family. These children will have double ordinal birth orders which will be different than the double birth orders that carry the only characteristics. These children with double birth orders, have a more complex personality, the product of the two birth orders. This "hidden" factor of two birth orders is just beginning to be understood and should give parents one more thing to consider when planning their families.

15

COMBINED OR BLENDED FAMILIES

STEPFAMILIES: **THE BRADY BUNCH** SITUATION

What dynamics come into play when children end up in a stepfamily? With the divorce rate so high in our country, the stepfamily is becoming the norm instead of the exception. A blended family or stepfamily occurs when parents get divorced or widowed and then remarry. If both parents bring their children into the new household, a blended family is created. This is the classic Brady Bunch family we saw on our television screens in the 1970s.

"Blended" is a poor word to describe this type of family. It's almost as bad as using the term "middle child" to describe the second child. For example, when we blend something in cooking, we change its texture, taste, or both. This is not the case when children are brought together in this new combined family. Children will strongly resist losing their identity and will try very hard not to blend. Some definitions are in order before we continue:

Siblings—biologically related; from the same parents
Stepsiblings—not biologically related; parents are married to each other

Half-siblings—partially biologically related; share one parent

Mutual child—a child born to the remarried couple

Residential stepchildren—live in the new household with the remarried parents most of the time

Non-residential stepchildren—live in the new household less than half the time

The U.S. Census Bureau sheds some light on marriage and divorce, and the odds on staying married don't look too good. We can only estimate current numbers, as the census stopped providing this information after 1990.

Current estimates show that 62 percent of all first marriages will end in a legal divorce. Always ready to try again, 75 percent of divorced persons will remarry. Of these remarriages, 43 percent have at least one of the adults coming from a divorce. Stepfamilies are formed 65 percent of the time as these remarriages involve children. Now here comes the bad statistic: 60 percent of these remarriages end in another legal divorce.

In my office we have had to adapt our computer programs to accept three or more names for many of our patients. Some of the children keep the name of the first family, so it's very common to have two names for each family. If mom decides to go back to her maiden name, then we get three names.

The Census Bureau gives us information on where children were living in the 2003 Current Population Survey. The findings show that 69 percent of children lived with two parents. Families where the mother is the only parent made up 23 percent; the father alone was 5 percent, and "someone else" was 3 percent. All these numbers mean that 31 percent of children live in a family without their two biological parents. If this trend continues, the combined family, where both parents bring children, is on the increase.

I can attest to this fact, for I have seen this trend in my office.

Adding a Piranha to a Fish Tank

When two sets of children are combined into one family, it's no summer camp. They know this is it for life....or is it? The dynamics go like this: If the child keeps his original birth order from the first family, then his adjustment will usually be fine. If he gets demoted in rank by an older child from the other family, then things don't go so well. This is the child about whom the step-parent may say to his mate: "I don't know why your child can't adjust to our new family. Mine have done fine." Talk about sparks getting ready to fly! No one likes to get demoted, and it's like getting salt poured in a wound when, after losing your first family, your position is lowered in the new family.

I can recall two families in my practice that tried to do a combination. He was a widower with three children; she a divorcée with an only child. The bond between a parent and an only child is always special and strong. This child becomes a confidant to the parent and is always asked for their opinion. Ashley wanted a new daddy, as her biological father would have nothing to do with her and her mother. She initially saw her stepfather as a plus in her life, so she went along with her mom on the marriage. What she didn't foresee was her new relationship in the combined family. Ashley, the only child, suddenly found herself fourth in line in the new family. What a demotion! She went from an only, on par with the adults, to the baby of the household. This new birth order is as far apart from her own as you can get. She didn't like the idea of sharing a bedroom and convinced her mom not to sell their house. In addition, she now had to share her best friend, her mom, with three other children and her new stepfather. She felt it was just fine to visit her new family, but she was not going to live there! When I talked with Ashley in the office I could sense she wanted everything back to the way it was before her mother remarried.

The TV Family—The Brady Bunch

The Brady Bunch premiered on September 26, 1969, and ran until August 30, 1974. The family was formed by the marriage of a widow with three girls to a widower with three boys. The six children ranged in age from seven to fourteen years. What we know about birth order in each family was that there was a one, a two, and a three of each sex. With the new combined family, some of the children kept their original birth orders, some moved up, and others moved down.

Greg, the oldest boy, kept his number-one position. Marcia, the oldest girl, formerly the number one in her family,

The Brady Bunch

moved down to the number-two position. Peter, the number-two boy, moved down to the three position. Jan, the number-two girl, moved down to the number-four position. Bobby, the number-three boy, moved to the number-five position, which is a second-level number one, so he saw a move up in birth order. Last there was Cindy, who started in the number-three position and was changed to a number six. A six birth order is really a second-level number two—a move up in birth order for her.

For those of you who followed this series, can you see the individual birth orders in the personalities of the children?

New Child to the Combined Family

Many times, after two families are united, the couple decides to add another child to the new family. This child is usually much younger than his or her half-siblings because of the time involved in divorce and remarriage.

One family that has been in the news is the family of Laci Peterson, who went missing Christmas Eve 2002. Her body (and that of her unborn child) washed up onto the eastern shore of San Francisco Bay. Laci's husband, Scott, was convicted of the murders. Due to the intense media interest in this story, we got a look at Scott's childhood and family. He was the seventh child in the combined family, which was a combination of his mother's prior three children and his father's prior three children.

Scott was the only child from the new marriage, the mutual child. He was the seventh child, but because of the years between him and his half-

Scott Peterson

siblings he also falls under the only child category. This would make him a seven/only, or he could be considered a three/only. All of his half-siblings said they spoiled him—one of his half-sisters said he was slow to walk because it wasn't necessary for him to learn, as he was always being carried around.

As a three/only, he has the influences of both the three and only birth orders on his personality. The drama, self-centeredness, and controlling personality that can sometimes be expressed in the three/only were evident in Scott. In the chapter on three/onlies we mentioned how good they are at manipulating others. Their appearance as a kind, understanding, gentle person can be overshadowed by the self-centered traits of the only. Laci was very taken with him, as were others. The jury just couldn't understand how he could be having an affair with another woman during his wife's pregnancy and after she was dead. He used his ability to understand others to control them and situations. He finally went too far.

FINAL THOUGHTS ON CHILDREN IN COMBINED FAMILIES

Look carefully at the birth orders of the children in their first family. Did they retain their original birth orders, move up, or get demoted? This will determine how well they will adjust to their new home. Also check the amount of time they spend living in the new arrangement. They may be nonresidents in the new house and would then be able to keep their old birth orders. Look out for the new child who may be born into this family. He may upset the dynamics between all members by having a very special place biologically. On the other hand, he may help bind the family together.

16

FACTORS AFFECTING CHANGES IN BIRTH ORDER

CHANGING YOUR BIRTH ORDER

Any change in birth order should be approached with caution. Most of the time these changes take place without our permission, through the death or a disabling accident of a sibling. Many times a medical problem can surface during childhood that disrupts the birth order balance by giving one sibling more attention. Sometimes we can see the change coming, as with a divorce and remarriage when the children are brought into a new combined home. When a dethroning of a first-born occurs as the result of sibling rivalry, it can have numerous repercussions that last a lifetime. The dethroned child resents the younger sibling who took his place, and the younger sibling has a new and larger role to play in the family.

Winning the sibling war can bring new responsibilities to the victor, and he may find that victory may not be so sweet. Whenever someone moves up or down in birth order, he still keeps many of the characteristics of his original birth order. This is the little extra baggage that happens with a change in birth order.

FAMILIES WITH CHILDREN WITH MEDICAL PROBLEMS

If a child in the family has a severe medical problem, whether at birth or later during childhood, the younger children will move up past this child in birth order. The oldest child may feel resentment toward this child as it reduces his role as the number-one attention recipient.

I know a woman whose younger sister was born with mental retardation. Throughout her childhood, she could not assert her number one birth order for attention. It was always about her sister. Growing up she was both an excellent student and athlete, taking both the roles of a number one and number two birth order. As an adult she appears to others to have a chip on her shoulder and a very caustic personality.

John Ritter

John Ritter, known for his role as Jack in the sitcom *Three's Company*, was born in 1948. He had an older brother, Tom, born in 1947. Tom was born with cerebral palsy and John took on the role of protector of his older brother. This was a very gentle dethroning with very little sibling rivalry, as John was born so soon after Tom. He probably never really felt that he was the younger brother, as he had the number one role from birth. In interviews Tom has said that John really took on the position of the older brother and protected him at school. Tom would watch from the audience as John performed with their dad, the country singer Tex Ritter.

Barbara Walters

Some moves up are not so smooth. Newswoman Barbara Walters has a fascinating childhood story, as she moved up from a third-born to a number-one position. The oldest child, a boy, died at age two, before she was born. The second child, Jackie, was mentally retarded. In 1931, Barbara was the third birth but moved up to the first-born position because of her brother's death and her sister's handicap. As a child she was very shy, typical of a third-born. The family was quite wealthy, as her dad started the Latin Quarter clubs, a chain of prestigious night clubs in Boston, New York, and Miami Beach. As a teenager, Barbara went to the best schools and had access to celebrities at her father's clubs. However, while Barbara was still a young woman, her father's gambling lost the family fortune. Barbara became a ruthless competitor, much like a second-born, as she had to help support the family. After her father died, she was the sole support for her mother and sister Jackie. We all know her television personality and how fearless an interviewer she can be. She has been married three times and has one adopted daughter, named after her sister Jackie. Currently she is the hostess of the women's forum program *The View*, where she can really express her opinions.

THE DEATH OF A SIBLING

This applies to both children and adults. When all of the children are adults and an adult older sibling dies, all the younger brothers and sisters move up in birth order. They still keep their original birth orders but must assume another role in the family structure. You might say they have acquired another birth order when it comes to their family.

This could be like a limited power of attorney, limited for use only within the family. When a child in the family dies, all the younger children also move up in birth order, each getting an additional birth order. This event can be more difficult for a family if the death occurs at an early age. When a death happens before the second child is born, the first child can be a phantom sibling if the parents have not accepted his death. Many times one or both parents don't resolve their grief over the death of this child and it really affects the next born child.

Cary Grant

This situation could have been the case with actor Cary Grant, born Archibald Alexander Leach in 1904. He was preceded by a brother who died as an infant. When Cary was nine years old, his mother had a mental breakdown and was sent to an asylum. Cary was then raised by his father as an only child.

George Walker Bush

Some families are faced with tragedy. This was especially the case of President George Walker Bush's family. He was the first child born to George and Barbara Bush on July 6, 1946. His sister, Pauline Robinson Bush, was born in 1949. The family called her Robin. Jeb Bush arrived on February 11, 1953. Eight months later, Robin's life was cut short by leukemia, two months shy of her fourth birthday, on October 11, 1953.

After the death of Robin and the birth of Jeb, George Walker found himself seven years older than his next younger sibling, Jeb. This was a change to his birth order—he went from a true number one to a one/only. This new birth order put him more in touch with adults. Barbara said she heard her son tell his friends he couldn't come out to play because he had to play with his mother, who was lonely. Barbara recalled, "Well, I'm being there for him. But the truth was he was being there for me." One of his uncles remarked on the "adult-like" manner in which George accepted the death of his sister.

Bill Cosby

Comedian Bill Cosby was born July 12, 1937, the oldest of four children.

Bill Cosby

He, like George Walker Bush, was the first-born. When Bill was eight years old, his younger brother by two years, James, died of rheumatic fever. The loss of James increased the age difference between Bill and his younger siblings and moved him up from a one to a one/only. This change can age a person quickly, and problems can arise if he or she is not ready for the responsibility. This may have indeed been the case for Bill: it wasn't until later in life that he truly found himself. He dropped out of high school, but later went back and eventually earned his Ph.D. in education. He has since enjoyed great success as a comedian, actor, husband, and father.

Ray Charles

Jazz pianist Ray Charles Robinson, born September 23, 1930, was the older of two boys. He had a brother one year younger, named George. When Ray was about five years old, he saw his brother drown in a washtub. Ray then changed his birth order from a one to an only child. Two months after the drowning, Ray began to lose his sight to undiagnosed glaucoma. His mother sent him to a school for the blind in Florida and the rest is history.

John Kennedy

President John F. Kennedy was the second-born in his family of seven children. His older brother, Joe Kennedy Jr., was the apple of his father's eye. The pressure was really on Joe Jr., as the stories about the boys during their education show. While at Choate, a private boys' school, Joe Jr. was more than willing to obey the rules. As a first-born, he identified with the authorities. Jack, however, could not resist challenging the rules. He and twelve of his friends had a jeweler make Phi Beta Kappa pins with the addition of a shovel and the letters CMC, which stood for Choate Muckers Club. These were a parody of the keys worn by the faculty. This led to a threat to expel the club members, but the headmaster thought better of it. Jack, as the happy-go-lucky number two, tried not to take anything too seriously, while Joe Jr. acted like a big brother and tried to keep Jack in line. Joe Jr. was quick with his fists and, like a true first-born, wanted to let little brother know who was boss. He would say to Jack, "When Dad's not here I'm the boss," and would then hit him to make his point. Joe Sr. had mapped out a plan for Joe Jr. to get into politics and become the first Catholic president of the United States. When Joe Jr. was killed when his plane was shot down during World War II, Jack was elevated from the second-born to the first-born position, and thus stepped into Joe Sr.'s plan. As the first Catholic president of the United States, he never lost his number-two sense of humor, and the press loved him.

Richard Nixon

President Richard Milhous Nixon is another second-born who moved up in birth order after the death of an older brother. Richard was born January 9, 1913, the second of five sons in a Quaker family. His older brother, Harold—born in 1909—was afflicted with tuberculosis. Although the family had little money, they were able to send him away for treatment. Thus Richard became the oldest in the household for several years of his childhood. When Richard was twenty years old his older brother came home to celebrate their mother's birthday. Harold died that day and Richard had to give her his present. This was a heavy burden for Richard to bear, as he moved up to the number-one position.

Nixon was a tough football player and a gifted student. Even though he had gotten a scholarship to Harvard, there was no money to cover outside expenses, so he had to settle for the local Whittier Community College. He tried even harder to be a perfect son following his brother's death. Moving up in birth order isn't always easy. Later he won a scholarship to the Duke University School of Law, where he graduated third in his class. Seven years after entering politics, he was elected vice president of the United States under General Dwight D. Eisenhower. Later he became the thirty-seventh president of the United States. He is the only person to be elected twice to the offices of vice president and president, and the only president to resign from office.

Katharine Hepburn

Actress Katharine Hepburn was born into a family of privilege. Her father, Dr. Thomas Norval Hepburn, a graduate of Johns Hopkins Medical School, was a urologist/surgeon who pioneered the use of contraceptives to fight venereal disease. This was a topic that was absolutely unmentionable in the early 1900s, but he fought for its public recognition and treatment. His wife, Katharine Houghton, campaigned for legal birth control and led the battle for women's suffrage. The year was 1907, and when little Katharine was old enough, she would march with her mother at the rallies for women's rights. There were six children in the family and Katharine was the second-born. Her brother Tom was the first-born.

Katharine Hepburn

A tragedy occurred during a weekend trip to visit their aunt in Greenwich Village. One morning Tom didn't come downstairs for breakfast, and Katharine went up to his room. She found him hanging from a beam. He was fourteen years old. Their mother never spoke his name again.

The event affected Katharine deeply, as evidenced by her behavior. She adopted Tom's birthday, November 8, as her own. She wore her hair like a boy and was known to go by "Jimmy." She refused to go back to school, so the rest of her education was completed at home. She always liked a challenge and was open about her lifelong affair with Spencer Tracy. Sandwiched between boys, she always took on a masculine approach to life. She was forceful and outspoken: even her penchant for wearing slacks and sneakers while other women wore stockings and high heels showed her rebel number two birth order and some two traits that she kept all her life.

Arnold Schwarzenegger

Arnold "The Terminator" Schwarzenegger, famous actor and governor of California, was born the second son to a policeman father. His brother,

Minehart, was just under four years older than he was. As is the case with many second-borns, Arnold excelled at sports. He came to America to find his fortune and used bodybuilding as his ticket. At age twenty, he became the youngest Mr. Universe. While in America, he learned of his older brother's death in a car accident in 1971. Arnold was twenty-three. He was now an only child, and with the death of his father in 1972, he became the head of his family.

He got a degree in economics from the University of Wisconsin in 1979, became a citizen in 1983, and married into the Kennedy family. Now he is leading the state of California as governor. He has his eyes set on the presidency and on changing the U.S. Constitution to allow foreign-born citizens the chance to hold the position. He is a great example of a second child who successfully moved into the only child position.

DETHRONING IN SIBLING RIVALRY

Sibling rivalry is another cause of movement in birth order. The dethroning of an older sibling is one of the most common forms of birth order change. The most common birth order rivalry is between first- and second-borns. Perhaps this is because the first-born position is so powerful that number two wants to fight for some of the power. After winning this position, the evolved number two still shows many of his second-born characteristics.

It's important to note that the first-born wants power and authority over others and views it as his birthright. The second-born does not want to be told what to do, so money, not power, is typically his goal. In some cases he may get the power along with the money, two qualities that make for a very interesting leader. In many cases the dethroning is by a male second-born over his first-born sister. He then takes on the typical characteristics of a first-born. Here are some examples of these dethroners:

Bob Dole

Former U.S. senator and presidential candidate Robert Joseph Dole was the second-born in his family. His older sister, Gloria, was born two years before him. Bob demonstrated the athletic ability typical of the second-born; he ran track and played basketball and football in high school. He served in the 10th Mountain Division during World War II, where he was seriously injured trying to rescue one of his men. He became a very powerful member of the U.S. Senate and then won the Republication nomination for the presidential election of 1996. Known to be a straight-shooting man of his word, he also has a great sense of humor and self-deprecation, as evidenced by his appearance in several humorous television commercials after the loss of his presidential bid—from Pepsi to Viagra.

Martin Luther King Jr.

Martin Luther King Jr. was a man of great principles and was the leader of the civil rights movement in our country. He was born two years after his sister, Christine. He was a man of strong convictions, and the stubborn two side of his personality came out when he refused to back down and compromise his ideas and goals. He became a lightning rod for all those who did not agree with him, and it cost him his life. It is interesting to note that his father was also the second-born with an older sister, as is his son, Martin Luther King III. This made the move up and the dethroning of the girls almost a natural occurrence in each generation.

Warren Buffett

We can't ignore the richest person in the United States, the "Oracle of Omaha," Warren Buffett. Mentioned earlier as an example of an independent number two, the president and CEO of Berkshire Hathaway turned the company into an investment business. He owns the insurance companies Geico and General Re and is the biggest shareholder of Coca-Cola. A single share of his Berkshire Hathaway stock, which he has refused to split, sells at over $120,000 per share. Warren is the second-born, with a sister two years older. Are you beginning to see the pattern of the male second child unseating his older sister? The second child's focus is on obtaining money—not for personal gain but for financial freedom.

Warren started his entrepreneurial career early. He and a friend started making money any way they could. This number two is also a man of his convictions: during the late 1990s tech stock frenzy, he said he didn't understand "dotcoms" and that he wouldn't buy

Warren Buffett

into them. It turned out he was right: the bubble burst and he and his company looked like prophets. He recently gave the Bill Gates Foundation the majority of his wealth to use for humanitarian purposes. Looks like similar birth orders have a natural affinity for trusting each other and believing in charity.

Rupert Murdoch

Keith Rupert Murdoch, the self-made billionaire media mogul, is a second-born. His sister, Helen, is two years his senior. Rupert is head of News Corporation, which owns numerous newspapers and television channels. He is quiet, a ruthless competitor, and is known to be conservative and controlling. If money has allowed this number two freedom from others telling him what to do, he has achieved his goal.

17

BECOMING A
BIRTH ORDER SLEUTH

BIRTH ORDER CLUES

Having an interest in birth order is an easy opening to any conversation. Everyone loves to talk about themselves and their families. This is great for me, as it has given me many opportunities to test my theories and refine the attributes of the various birth orders.

As I wrote the earlier chapters, I was looking forward to writing this last chapter—the chapter of stories I've heard over the years about families. Now that you have learned about the various birth orders, you can share with me how "Life's Fingerprint" works. Here are a few more stories about birth orders, some ordinary people and some everyone knows. As you become a birth order sleuth, you will be able to pick up the subtle shadings in people's birth orders.

TENNIS, ANYONE?

While waiting for my tennis partner I had the opportunity to strike up a conversation with another fellow also waiting for his partner. Ted was an outgoing, happy guy and told me how he cherished his time away from home. I guessed that he was a later-born child, and I said, "I bet you have older brothers or sisters?"

Surprised, he said, "How did you know that?"

Without going into too much detail, I said, "Well, it looks like you can have a conversation with anyone and you like people."

"Boy, is that true," he said. "I have an older brother and older sister. She's the oldest."

"Are you just a few years apart?"

He said yes, and I delved deeper to learn that he sold laundry equipment for a living. He was the type of man who was comfortable calling on new clients. He told me that he could sense in just a matter of minutes whether they were going to buy. I told him it was a great job that really fit his birth order as a three.

As we continued our conversation, I guessed that his wife was the first-born in her family. "Boy, are you good," he said. "Are you a psychiatrist?" It looks like he matched his childhood birth order by marrying a girl who was the same order as his older sister.

He then said, "If you're so good at this, let me tell you about my dad and his family. Dad was the first-born and then three years later twin girls were born. One of them had some medical problems. She died in her forties and Dad still won't talk to the other twin."

"What did his father, your grandfather, do?" I asked.

"Oh, he was a professional musician and was gone a lot, so Dad, I guess, filled the male role in the family."

This one was easy to figure out, but only because one of the twins was ill all her life. The father, a first-born, was threatened by the twins because of all the attention they got at his expense. Next, he had to play a protective role as the oldest male in the house with his father on the road. His special position was threatened even more when one of the twins became ill and took a lot of the family resources and attention. Because of her illness, there was no way he could fight the other twin to keep his top position and attention. To this day, he will not speak to the one surviving twin, and she is at a loss as to the reason. We know as birth order sleuths that it was just an act of birth. I'm sure the man isn't even aware of these underlying factors. His responses to his family throughout his life were just unconscious reactions to his surroundings.

THE ELECTRICIAN GETS MARRIED

My electrician is one of the happiest guys I know. We always hit it off when he comes by, and I really like his sense of humor. I found out that he is the sixth-born in his family. Being a second-born myself, we have a lot in common. (Remember, a sixth-born is a second-level two.) With a guy this happy, I just had to know about his wife and kids. He said he married a woman six years older than himself and she already had four daughters. They did not have any children together. (As a sixth-born, he would be comfortable with an older mate, as the arrangement duplicated his own childhood situation with much older sisters.) Things have not always gone smoothly for this couple, as he told me they had twice filed for divorce, but they got back together both times. I told him she must be a special lady. He agreed. It's tough to break the birth order bonds that mimic your childhood relationships.

EVERYBODY LOVES RAYMOND?

The family depicted in the television sitcom *Everybody Loves Raymond* expresses classic sibling rivalry and the birth order switch. For those of you not familiar with the program, it portrayed a dysfunctional family situation. Raymond, the younger son, is married with children, is a successful sportswriter, and lives next door to his parents, who are always dropping by. His overbearing mother, Marie, continually involves herself where she doesn't belong and treats him as her favorite son. Raymond's older brother, Robert, is divorced, is a detective with the police force, and has one failed relationship after another, with a little help from his well-meaning mother. His parents are always saying, "Why can't you be more like Raymond?" Raymond has clearly taken over Robert's number-one position. And every time Robert is put down by his family, he sighs with dissatisfaction, "Everybody loves Raymond."

CHANGING BIRTH ORDER THROUGH
NEW LIVING ARRANGEMENTS

I met Debbie and her boyfriend on vacation a number of years ago. They had been backpacking in the White Mountains of New Hampshire and were on their way to do a little whitewater kayaking. Debbie was born an only child—less athletically competitive—so all this physical activity just didn't add up.

After her father died when she was three years old, Debbie and her mother went to live with her aunt and cousins. The two cousins were a girl six months older than Debbie and a boy two years younger. This made Debbie a functional number two who would develop her athletic skills along with her academic work. She never understood why she was so athletically oriented when her mother was not. We know that her mother had nothing to do with her interest in athletics—it was her new birth order position. She had to find a way to be different from her older cousin, who was more like an older sister. This living arrangement also affected Debbie's current social life, as her boyfriend was a third-born (same order as her younger male cousin) who had an older sister, thus mimicking both their childhood birth orders.

LOVE ON THE INTERNET

With the explosion of Internet dating services, you can get a glimpse of someone's personal history and what he or she wants in a mate by reading profile advertisements. These ads can be quite candid and revealing. As "Life's Fingerprint" comes into view, the person's birth order can be obvious. For example, "Lisa" said in her profile,

> I started out as a schoolteacher but spent most of my time working in the drama department. I also performed for three years as an actress. I was a model and a singer. People all say I'm better-looking than most women my age and also smarter. I've always said, if I find the right man I'd lock him in a closet and only let him out when I needed him, ha ha. I have two cats and two dogs. I love to dance, hate boring people, and refuse to grow old. My older brothers say I'm too picky, but the man I want should be very bright, neat in appearance and habits, have a sense of humor, love nature, animals, and all people regardless of age, sex, occupation, religion, or race. My two older brothers are six and eight years older than me.

You have it right, this lady has the double birth order of a three/only. Did you pick up the three's typical interest in the arts, such as her acting, dancing, and singing? The love of nature, animals, and openness to others and new ideas are also traits of the third-born. Being the only girl in the family with two older brothers, she has always felt special and was treated that way. As the baby she refuses to grow old, but the only side of her birth order makes her very specific in what she wants. Her little joke about locking her man in a closet shows just how much she wants to be in control—and may not be much of a joke. The three/only can be the drama queen, and you sense the feeling of the dramatic with this person.

MOM REALLY WANTED A **BIG** FAMILY, BUT TRIPLETS?

With the advent of successful family planning, there are not too many families that include more than four children. A friend of mine is from a family of eight children, and when she heard I was writing a book on birth order, she volunteered information about her family.

The complexity of this large family will confirm what we have learned. All the children were no more than three years apart, and all were boys except for the third-born, my friend Jan. The sixth birth was triplets! Now I know why Jan felt so special. As the only girl with seven brothers, it didn't take much for her to stand out. Jan is a teacher and school administrator, a perfect fit for a three—dealing with groups and helping to educate the world.

The oldest boy became an airline pilot—number one is a very common birth order among pilots.

The second boy became a history teacher and left his hometown. He couldn't compete with his older brother, who was quite the student and athlete; there was no birth order switch here. His younger sister, being the only girl, really stifled his individuality (not her fault, of course), and so he felt that he had to leave town to make his own way.

The fourth boy works in the personnel department of the city transit company and is well liked by everyone. He loves to write comedy and his peers think he could be a stand-up comedian. He follows in the fourth child's path as the real cut-up in the family, always craving attention.

With the fifth-born we get another number one, but of the second level. This boy got his MBA and is now vice president of a national food company. Another very good match, as this second-level number one likes to give orders. His sister said he was very competitive growing up.

Last come the triplets, numbers six, seven, and eight. They put a lot of pressure on number five for the family's attention. Six would be a second-level number two. He also left his hometown, just like his number two brother. Number seven is a second-level number three. He is a very people-oriented type of person. He knows everyone and is the guy to see when you want those special tickets no one else can get. He is also the child who is taking care of their mother in her old age. This is the sensitive side of the number three who really cares about others. The last brother, number eight, is a second-level four. He has the gift of gab and directed it into law. He went to night school while working and raising a family. He is now working with large groups of defendants in his law practice, another gift that would come easily to a number eight.

FAMILY WITHIN A FAMILY

The television sitcom *Malcolm in the Middle* depicts a "family within a family" birth order sequence. The oldest boy, Francis, is many years older than his next three brothers, making him a one/only. Reese is the oldest of the next three boys, a 2/1. The next child is Malcolm, in the middle of this second family as a 3/2, hence the name of the show. Last is Dewey, who is

Malcolm in the Middle

a 4/3. Linwood Boomer, the show's writer, based the family on his own real-life experience.

Francis, the one/only, is sent off to military school. The second child, Reese, is not very bright and is an athlete and a bully. His athleticism and bullish tendencies are characteristics of both a two and a one, his double birth order. Malcolm is a genius who just doesn't fit in. Malcolm's birth order, 3/2, is really a complicated one and it shows in the sitcom.

There is also a birth order shift in this second family between Reese and Malcolm, as the older brother is usually better in school, which is not the case in their situation. The youngest, Dewey, the 4/3, is really the baby in the family. He pulls all the tricks that only a baby can do to his older brothers. He really understands their motives, but he does not compete with them.

STEPFAMILIES CHANGE CHILDREN'S BIRTH ORDERS

When visiting a print shop in my town, I noticed the two clerks, women in their thirties, having way too much fun. Each was punching the other in the arm, joking around and talking loudly. When it was my turn, I moved to the front of the line and said, "I'll bet the two of you had three older brothers or sisters?" (The loud talking and playful punching can be number-four traits.) One woman said that she was the fourth child and the other said she was the sixth. This didn't add up, so I asked the clerk who said she was the sixth, "how many children were in your family?" She said there were eleven, and further explained that the two oldest children were her half-siblings who had not lived with the family while she was growing up. Hence the discrepancy. She was really a functional number four. Her story is a perfect example of why it is important to ask questions and dig deeper if things don't seem to add up.

A BIG FAMILY WITH CHILDREN SPACED FIVE YEARS APART

The mother of one of my patients was the fifth and last child in her family. The oldest was the only boy and was nine years older than the oldest sister. All four girls were five years apart in age. As adults the girls decided to take a trip each year to keep their family ties together. It's difficult to really connect with your siblings when you're all five years apart. Instead of a close family of children, each child is raised as an individual only-child family. This five year separation means that the girls all had double birth orders of 2/0, 3/0, 4/0, and 5/0. The 5/0 is really a type of 1/0. The last child's complaint was that every year she had to do all the planning for the trip. She couldn't understand why her older sisters just didn't have a clue about getting anything done. As she describes them, the 2/0 is a princess and expects everyone to cater to her. The 3/0 makes a scene about everything and is dramatic and disorganized. The 4/0 is totally lost but thinks she has it all together up until the moment things fall apart.

I explained to her that although she was the youngest, she was more like a first-born and thus had the most skill at getting things done. It was like a light went off in her head and she really started to see her sisters' unique qualities.

THEY TOOK OUT MY APPENDIX

I met two brothers from Germany while I was on vacation. I remarked at how fluent they were in English, and they said they had been educated in England. They were born during World War II, and after the war, their parents felt they should go to England to learn English. They were separated and sent to different families.

One brother told a story that immediately revealed his birth order. He was ten years old when he was sent to England. He could not speak much English and speaking German in England after the war did not engender a warm welcome at his new school. He became very homesick and devised a plan to return home. He thought if he feigned a terrible stomachache, he would be sent home to Germany. But things did not work out as planned. The family with whom he was living contacted his parents, who gave the okay to take him to the hospital. Once at the hospital, he still would not give in and confess that he was faking. I asked, "Did you get home?" He said, "Before I knew it, they took me in for surgery and took out my appendix! I knew then that I had to do whatever my parents wanted."

Did you figure out his birth order? He wanted to control his own space and would not give in. He is a second-born.

18

BIRTH ORDER IN THE WORKPLACE

I LOVE MY JOB—JUST NOT THE PEOPLE I WORK WITH

Now that you know about birth order and your siblings, combined families, and marriage partners, it's time to examine the workplace. The early "fingerprint" of the time spent with siblings will carry over to the workplace as fellow workers become in a sense adopted siblings. Interactions with coworkers often resemble sibling relationships, especially among those who have the same birth orders as your siblings.

For a number of years I lectured to audiences of orthodontic office staff, following up with a survey. I was trying to discover which birth orders naturally gravitate to specific positions in the orthodontic office. The orthodontic office staff can be divided into several clearly delineated positions. Front desk staff deals with the parents, make appointments, collect money, and answer the phone. Chairside staff assists in the technical work, working directly with the doctor and patients. Laboratory staff makes many of the appliances for the patients. The laboratory is usually isolated from the rest of the office.

My surveys always asked what positions respondents had held, and for how long. I also asked for the total number of years they had worked for an orthodontist. My reasoning was that certain birth orders naturally moved to positions where they were most comfortable, even if they had been initially trained for another. If particular birth orders were best suited for certain positions, it would help both doctors and staff if everyone started off in their ideal jobs.

Here is what I found: Onlies and first-borns worked best at the front desk position. Their personalities are strong enough to enforce the office rules for appointments and collections. They interacted well with parents on the phone and in person. They just loved being in charge and running the show. The chair side assistants were overwhelmingly third- and fourth-borns who loved interaction in a group environment. It didn't bother them that many different things were going on around them. This may be similar to the experiences they had with all their siblings when they were growing up.

The laboratory staff were mostly second-borns who loved to control their own space, with few people telling them what to do.

YOUR WORKPLACE

Not everyone has the desire or the opportunity to be the boss. Most people have a supervisor that came with the job. The supervisor may have been promoted because he or she was doing a lower-level job well and someone in charge felt it was time for a move up. This is not necessarily always a successful move. Not everyone wants the added responsibility or the burden of directing others.

Each birth order has its own style, and the workplace seems to run more smoothly if the highest birth order is on top. Find out your supervisor's birth order and see how it relates to yours. Each birth order has its way of coping with authority. You may not enjoy taking orders from someone you sense has a lower birth order. On the other hand, if a first-born is in charge, it's just like old times for them. Second-borns may use the same tactics that they did as children to confront their older sibling. Stubbornness and passive aggression come to mind.

Using your knowledge of birth order relationships can make your life at work easier! Now you will have a better feel for the office dynamics.

BIRTH ORDER MANAGEMENT STYLES

Onlies and first-borns want to give orders and be in charge. Second-borns don't want to be told what to do and are more indirect in giving orders. Third-borns love the group interaction but may show a very stern, cold exterior as they try to protect their vulnerable inner selves. Once you get to know them, you will see their sweet, sensitive side. They really do understand your pain and want to help. Fourth-borns want to have fun, so it won't be all work and no play. Fourth-borns will try to make any job a game and their fellow employees a part of the team. They may also try to find someone to help them out, much like the help they got from their older siblings.

Management Styles Reflect the CEO's Birth Order

I have found that most major corporations have onlies and first-borns on their top management teams. There are a few exceptions that come to mind, which are examples of how the CEO's birth order can affect the company. Until recently, Bill Gates was the president of the Microsoft Corporation. Is it any wonder that many of his employees were independent contractors? As a second-born, Bill liked his independence and felt others would as well. As children Bill and his siblings, his older sister and younger sister, competed in almost everything they did. It's easy to see how this behavior translated to his adult life and the business world. We can see his stubborn number-two side in his antitrust suit against the federal government. Second-borns can use their money to buy their freedom. They just don't like other people telling them what they can and cannot do.

Bill Gates

Who hasn't flown on Southwest Airlines? This airline has rewritten the book on how we travel and how airline employees behave. Does having fun come to mind? Well, founder and CEO Herb Kelleher is an only/four. We know the fourth child likes to have fun, so it's no surprise that Herb has added a little humor to the hassle of air travel. For years Southwest did not assign seats: placement was first come, first-served—much like a large family at dinnertime. When the flight attendant says the smoking section is out on the wing, you know you're not on any of the other airlines.

POLITICS: PRESIDENTS, VICE PRESIDENTS, AND CABINET MEMBERS

Let's take a closer look at some of the people our presidents have selected to work with them. It might surprise you how much birth order comes into play.

Richard Nixon was a second son who moved up to the number-one position after the death of his older brother. He chose Spiro Agnew as his running mate. Agnew was a two/only. Was this second-born position what drew Nixon to him? Agnew ended up leaving office early because of a scandal. The early end of Nixon's presidency was the Watergate affair—the break-in of the Democratic election committee headquarters and its subsequent cover-up. I'm sure these scandals weren't related to birth order. The fact that Nixon and Agnew both were second-borns made for some character similarities and allowed Agnew to be the willing attack dog when confronting the press for Nixon.

Jimmy Carter is a first-born. He chose as his vice president another first-born, Walter Mondale. This may be stretching it a little, as Walter had a half-brother who was twenty-four years older. Walter was the first-born in his father's second family; his half-brother was already an adult.

Ronald Reagan, a second-born with an older brother, chose George H. W. Bush for his vice president. George was also a second-born with an older brother. Alexander Haig Jr. was his first secretary of state. He is a two/only with an older sister and a much younger little brother. Colin Powell, head of the Joint Chiefs of Staff under George H. W. Bush, is a two/only birth order with a sister five years older. All these men had the two birth order represented in their "fingerprint." The two men that were two/onlies were the most outspoken during their terms. I'm sure it was the function of the only side of their birth orders.

Bill Clinton, an only/one, chose as his running mate Al Gore, an only/two. Both men clung tightly to their beliefs and didn't seem to work well as a team. Not surprising for two people with strong only tendencies!

George W. Bush is a first-born who moved up to become a one/only after the death of his younger sister. He picked Dick Cheney as his vice president. A very experienced politician, Cheney is also a first-born. The two of them are more alike then anyone knows. Bush's first secretary of state was Colin L. Powell, a two/only who didn't get along very well with the team. We can see why: as a two/only he needs to control his own space and not be told what to do. He left the administration after the first term and was succeeded by Condoleezza Rice, an only child. She fit much better with Bush and Cheney. Former secretary of defense Donald Rumsfeld is a number two. He didn't mind working in the support role for the president, as he made his own decisions at the Department of Defense. Rumsfeld showed the stubborn side of the two birth order in his frequent confrontations with the press and views on the Iraq war. He too has left the administration.

Now you can take a fresh look at you own work situation. Are you a manager with many people to coordinate into a team? Do you want to be an owner someday and have to hire people for various positions in your company? The birth order of these employees will make a difference in your company's success. If you are one of the "worker bees," is this the job for you? Does it fit your birth order and what you like doing best? You can see the examples about the "tone" set by a company owner. Do you fit in or should you find another company or position that is a better fit for you?

19

FINAL THOUGHTS

I hope this book has clarified for you the concept of birth order and the way it affects your worldview and life path as well as your personality traits. Combination or double birth orders are the real Rosetta stone to understanding this whole concept. Most of the published work on birth order does not take this very important concept into account. Most explanations only use the ordinal, or number order of birth, in assigning traits to the various birth orders. Perhaps those researchers will modify their selection process and separate the Double Birth Orders so we can get more representative results in future surveys and experiments.

For those of you with growing children, please don't have the same expectations for each child. Let them show you their unique qualities—children are not all alike and they really don't want to be like their older siblings. Don't let your ego interfere with their individuality.

For teachers and other caregivers, do not treat all children alike, but look for those special birth order differences that will allow you to interact with them in a more effective way.

Last, for all of us, look to see how those around you still demonstrate their childhood birth orders. Birth order traits affect you as an employer, coworker, parent, friend, husband, wife, and on and on. If you use birth order theory to reason out the life paths around you, you will better understand peoples' diverse personalities and their "Life's Fingerprint."

ACKNOWLEDGMENTS

This should be the easiest section for me to write, but it is the hardest. There have been so many people who have contributed to this book—some aware, many unaware.

Ann Flannery, an only child, whose love of books and the written word is second only to her love of animals. I give her the credit for getting me to write the book.

Many of my friends have given me so much information. Liz and Dennis Berk and Jane Trull, friends who read the unfinished manuscript on numerous vacations and gave me invaluable suggestions. Now I won't be asking them to "look at the birth order book" this year.

Mary and Wade North and Joel and Jimmy Phillips, who each Thanksgiving gave me information on children from their very large families. My former college roommate Don Clewell reminded me that there may be a biologic ingredient to birth orders.

Faye and Ray Authement, whose children I watched grow up, get married, and have children of their own. As parents and grandparents, they shared with me many stories of their children and grandchildren that helped confirm my birth order theories.

Art Hickham, my friend and retired dentist who gave me the quote, "I worked once and I didn't like it." He is the fourth-born of four boys. He is now enjoying life visiting his grandchildren and riding his motorcycle.

Ron Hebert, a fellow orthodontist, who tried my theories in his practice and brainstormed with me on the specific characteristics of many of the double birth orders. It was he who reminded me that "there are no bad birth orders" just differences.

John and Gloria Barbour who showed me that any birth order combination can result in a long and happy marriage. Walter and Martha Culpepper both being second borns show the perpetual athleticism of the second-born.

To the men of our "Tuesday Lunch" group, Tom Carney, Brent MacDonald, Rob Lancaster, Richard Moore, and John Jackson for all the stories about your kids and families—many of which I have used in this book.

Thanks to my patient friends who have been waiting for this book: Dr. John Williams; Dr. Mindy Hickey; Dr. Lisa Pellegrini; Chester Wang; and Dr. Charlie and Mrs. Anne Foy.

My office staff, Anne Schroeder, Sharon Sailers, and Jennifer Arnoult, who worked with me and our patients as my theory of double birth orders worked itself out in the office. Of course, I can't forget all the patients who showed me variations between family members. Many of my patients gave me information on their birth orders when I was able to see them as adults. Without these patients and their wonderful real life stories, this book would be incomplete.

This book would not have been complete without the pictures of the children—children who are now all young adults. Thanks to the Knisely family: Erica, Josh and Mac; and to the Brossette girls: Bonnie, Kelly, Robin and Kristen.

Thanks to Werner and Heinz Adelt. Your stories always made me laugh, but each had a lesson about birth order. Too bad about Werner losing his appendix.

To Kristina Phillips, the designer of this book, who spent many hours getting all of the artistic portions of the book "just right." As a first-born, the details really count. Our cover truly reflects the various paths each of us must take to fulfill our birth orders. Raymond Calvert did the initial graphics for the book. Little did we know that Hurricane Katrina would submerge his computer in water, but fortunately not all of his work was lost.

A special thank you to Fina Flores for all her work on the graphics and layout and for the support from everyone at Llumina Press. The back cover design and final layout was done by Amber Colleran, a graphic artist who put the finishing touches on the book and made the graphics and photos come to life.

I can't forget all those people who had the misfortune to sit next to me on airplanes, who gave me their life stories, and let me talk with them about birth order, I apologize.

Last, how could I not thank my editor, Miriam Moore, for all her work in editing this book. As a fifth-born in a family of six, she had just the right approach to this second-born. I never found her suggestions to be anything but constructive. Her insight into how the information should be presented really made the book what it truly is: a guide to the use of birth order in your life.

FIND YOUR TRUE BIRTH ORDER QUESTIONNAIRE

1. List in order from oldest to youngest the names and ages of all your natural brothers and sisters. Include yourself and circle your name.

_____

_____

_____

This will give you your ordinal birth number. If there are four or more years between you and your nearest older and younger sibling (if present), you can add the only birth order to your ordinal one. (1/0, 2/0, 3/0, 4/0, etc.)

If there is a space of four years between your nearest older sibling and you and all other siblings are less than four years apart, then you are a family within a family (addressed in Chapter Eleven). If you are a child in a family within a family then you can add another ordinal number to your birth order.

The first sibling after the four-year gap would add a one. For example, if you were the third-born, have younger siblings, and there were four years between you and your older sibling, then you are a 3/1. Your next sibling would be a 4/2.

2. List in order from oldest to youngest the names and ages of all your stepbrothers and stepsisters. If any stepsiblings lived with you, list them in order by age and then refigure your ordinal birth order.

_____

_____

_____

3. Which of your natural siblings and which of your stepsiblings did you live with from birth to age sixteen?

_____

_____

_____

4. Did you ever live with adults other than your parents from birth to age sixteen? How many years did you live with these people?

    a) grandparents_____
    b) aunts or uncles_____
    c) close family friends_____
    d) other_____

This information will let you know if you get a new birth order due to separation from your other siblings. It must be a period longer than a year or two to make any difference.

5. If you answered yes to question #4, at what age did you live with these people? Were there other children in the house? If yes, list their ages and yours at the time you lived with them.

_____

_____

_____

6. Were any of your brothers or sisters (including stepbrothers and stepsisters) with whom you lived handicapped either mentally or physically? If so, which ones?

_____

7. Did any of your brothers or sisters die either before you were born or after? If so, which ones and how old were you at their time of death? If they were older than you, move up one number in birth order.

_____

_____

8. Were you adopted or did you have any adopted siblings in the family? Put everyone in order by their age and consider your age or theirs at the time of adoption.

_____

_____

9. Are you a twin or triplet? If so, are you the first-, second-, or third-born? Were there any siblings born before or after you and your twin or triplet? If so, how many years apart?

_____

_____

For more information and/or to contact Dr. Hurst,
please go to www.lifesfingerprint.com

INDEX